**GOOD HOUSEKEEPING**

# Best
# Dinner Parties

# GOOD HOUSEKEEPING

# Best Dinner Parties

EBURY PRESS
LONDON

Published in 1993 by Ebury Press
an imprint of Random House UK Ltd
Random House
20 Vauxhall Bridge Road
London SW1V 2SA

**COOKERY NOTE**
Follow either metric or imperial measures for the recipes in
this book as they are not interchangeable.

Catalogue record for this book is available from the British
Library.

ISBN: 0 09 177756 9

Editor: Helen Southall
Design: Christine Wood

Typeset by Textype Typesetters, Cambridge
Printed and bound in Italy by New Interlitho S.p.a., Milan

# CONTENTS

# INSTANT SUCCESS SUPPER

If you're out at work all day, or have a busy family schedule, time is at a premium, so we've devised a menu for which all the ingredients should be available in your local supermarket. We've also prepared two countdowns; you can either do most of the work the evening before or, if necessary, do everything on the night.

When time is really short, take advantage of any available short-cuts. Instead of making the Warm Lemon Bread, buy a chilled or frozen ready-to-bake garlic or herb baguette. Open it out and drizzle with a little lemon juice before you serve it. Good bottled French or vinaigrette dressings are now readily available – simply add chopped chives and olives to your favourite one to serve with the Artichoke and Ham Salad. Also a blessing for those in a hurry are bags of prepared mixed-leaf salads. These can be made more interesting by adding chopped spring onions, pine nuts, alfalfa sprouts or toasted nuts. Frozen puff pastry in ready-to-roll sheets thaws quickly and is easy to roll out.

*Artichoke and Ham Salad (page 8), Warm Lemon Bread (page 9)*

## —— PLAN-AHEAD COUNTDOWN ——

**The day before**

Mix together the artichoke, olives and dressing for the starter, and refrigerate. Toast the pine nuts and store in an airtight container. Prepare the Warm Lemon Bread as far as the end of step 1. Store in a cool place. Sauté the veal for the gratin. Leave to cool. Sauté the spinach and cool. Cook the pasta, drain well and cool. Make the sauce, cover with greaseproof paper and cool. Combine the pasta, spinach and veal. Keep the sauce separate. Cover both with cling film and refrigerate. Wash 12 small tomatoes. Make a small cross in the base of each, place in an oven-proof dish, cover and refrigerate. Make a dressing for the salad, if serving. Cover and store in a cool place. Thaw the pastry for the pudding.

**On the day**
**To serve at 8 pm**

**6 pm:** Prepare the garlic and courgettes for the Lamb with Rosemary, if serving. Prepare the watercress, lettuce and onion salad, if serving. Refrigerate in polythene bags. Prepare the pastry for the pudding as directed in step 1. Cover closely with cling film and refrigerate. Peel, halve and core the apples, and slice as directed. Place in a large bowl, cover with cold water and add lemon juice to prevent discolouration.

**6.30 pm:** Plate the Artichoke and Ham Salad. Cover and refrigerate.

**7 pm:** Drain and dry the apple halves and assemble the pastries to the end of step 3. Return to the fridge. Preheat the oven to 200°C (400°F) mark 6. Reheat the sauce for the gratin.

**7.30 pm:** Place the Warm Lemon Bread and the gratin in the oven to bake.

**7.45 pm:** Add a dash of vinegar and water to the tomatoes and bake for 10–12 minutes.

**8 pm:** Serve the meal. Increase the oven temperature to 240°C (475°F) mark 9 and put the pudding in to cook. Light the grill if serving Lamb with Rosemary.

## —— LAST-MINUTE COUNTDOWN ——

**To serve at 8 pm**

**5.45 pm:** Thaw the pastry and spinach. Prepare the gratin or the lamb, courgettes and garlic. Wash the salad ingredients. Make a dressing.

**6.30 pm:** Assemble the Artichoke and Ham Salad on individual serving dishes. Cover and refrigerate. Prepare the Warm Lemon Bread. Leave in a cool place. Prepare the tomatoes as described in the Plan-Ahead Countdown.

**7 pm:** Prepare the pudding to the end of step 3; refrigerate. Preheat the oven to 200°C (400°F) mark 6.

**7.30 pm:** Place the Warm Lemon Bread and the gratin in the oven to bake.

**7.45 pm:** Put the tomatoes on to bake.

**8 pm:** Serve the meal as directed in the Plan-Ahead Countdown. Light the grill if serving Lamb with Rosemary.

---

**FREEZER NOTES**

*The Gratin of Spinach and Veal will freeze if you cook the veal escalopes right through at step 1; sauté them for 3–4 minutes. Continue to the end of step 4. Cool, overwrap and freeze. To use, thaw overnight at cool room temperature, then bake as directed in the recipe. Do not freeze Lamb with Rosemary, the salads or the Caramelised Apple Wafer.*

---

# Artichoke and Ham Salad

*Prosciutto is the Italian word for ham, and prosciutto crudo is ham which has been air-dried, of which Parma is perhaps the best-known example.*

two 312 g (11 oz) cans artichoke hearts, drained
50 g (2 oz) pine nuts, toasted

90 ml (6 tbsp) olive oil
30 ml (2 tbsp) red wine vinegar
15 ml (1 level tbsp) snipped fresh chives (optional)
12 black olives, pitted and roughly chopped
black pepper
225 g (8 oz) *prosciutto crudo*, very thinly sliced
Warm Lemon Bread, to serve

1 Quarter the artichokes and put them in a medium mixing bowl. Stir in the pine nuts.
2 Whisk together the olive oil, red wine vinegar and chives, if using. Stir in the olives. Pour the dressing over the artichoke mixture and stir well. Season with pepper only, as the ham and olives will add enough salt.
3 Arrange the ham on individual dishes. Spoon over the artichoke mixture and the dressing. Serve with Warm Lemon Bread.

*210 Calories per serving*

---

⌇

# WARM LEMON BREAD

*The fresh lemon flavour of this bread perfectly complements the richness of the air-dried ham.*

1 medium crusty loaf
olive oil
juice of 1 lemon
black pepper

1 Cut the loaf into large chunks and place on a large sheet of foil. Drizzle over 60–90 ml (4–6 tbsp) olive oil and about 30 ml (2 tbsp) lemon juice. Season with lots of black pepper, then wrap tightly in the foil.
2 Heat in the oven at 200°C (400°F) mark 6 for about 25 minutes. Serve immediately.

*140 Calories per serving*

# GRATIN OF SPINACH AND VEAL

oil
6 veal or turkey escalopes, about 700 g (1½ lb) total weight
10 ml (2 level tsp) paprika
15 ml (1 tbsp) lemon juice
1 garlic clove, skinned and crushed
225 g (8 oz) frozen chopped spinach, thawed and drained
grated nutmeg
salt and pepper
350 g (12 oz) dried tagliatelle or tagliarini, or 450 g (1 lb) fresh
50 g (2 oz) butter
50 g (2 oz) plain flour
900 ml (1½ pints) milk
125 g (4 oz) full-fat soft cheese with garlic and herbs

1 Heat 30 ml (2 tbsp) oil in a shallow flame-proof casserole. Fry the veal escalopes, a few pieces at a time, with the paprika, until well browned. Drain and cut into strips.
2 Add the lemon juice, garlic and spinach to the pan. Sauté over a high heat, adding a little more oil if necessary, for 2–3 minutes. Season well with nutmeg, salt and pepper, then remove from the pan.
3 Meanwhile, cook the pasta in plenty of boiling, salted water. Drain and transfer to the casserole. Add the spinach and veal.
4 Melt the butter in a medium saucepan and stir in the flour. Cook, stirring, for 1–2 minutes before adding the milk. Bring to the boil, then simmer, stirring, for 3–4 minutes or until thickened. Off the heat, beat in the soft cheese and adjust the seasoning. Spoon over the veal.
5 Bake, uncovered, in the oven at 200°C (400°F) mark 6 for 35–40 minutes.

*480 Calories per serving*

# LAMB WITH ROSEMARY

*We used rosemary not only to flavour the meat but also as a 'skewer' for joining the thin end of each chop to the thicker part.*

12 large garlic cloves
450 g (1 lb) courgettes, sliced
olive oil
salt and pepper
6 lamb loin chops, about 175 g (6 oz) each,
trimmed of fat
long sprigs of fresh rosemary

1 Preheat the grill. Cook the unpeeled garlic cloves in boiling water for 5 minutes, then drain and arrange on the grill pan with the sliced courgettes. Brush with oil and season.
2 Bend the tail of each chop around the eye of the meat. Using a skewer, make holes through each chop and thread with rosemary sprigs to secure. Brush with oil.
3 Grill the garlic and courgettes for 5 minutes, stirring after 2 minutes. Add the lamb chops and grill for 8 minutes on each side. The garlic skin will blacken but the flesh inside will be soft and smoky.

*480 Calories per serving*

# CARAMELISED APPLE WAFER

*The tops of the apple slices and the pastry edges will look very dark.*

125 g (4 oz) chilled or frozen puff pastry, thawed
6 small Granny Smith apples, about 450–700 g
(1–1½ lb) total weight
75 g (3 oz) butter or margarine, melted
60 ml (4 level tbsp) demerara sugar
Greek-style natural yogurt, to serve

1 Halve the pastry, then, on a lightly floured surface, roll out very thinly to give two rectangles measuring about 20.5×11.5 cm (8×4½ inches). Trim the edges, then place on two baking sheets.
2 Peel and halve the apples, and remove the cores. Place the apple halves, rounded-side up, on a work surface and thinly slice them, but not quite through to the base. The apples should retain their shape. Evenly space six halves, flat-side down, on each pastry base to cover completely. Slice both rectangles into three.
3 Brush the apple with the butter and sprinkle over the demerara sugar.
4 Bake in the oven at 240°C (475°F) mark 9 for about 20 minutes or until the apples are soft and caramelised. Serve immediately with Greek-style natural yogurt.

*280 Calories per serving*

# CALIFORNIA-STYLE SUNSET SUPPER

---

## Menu

*Mixed Leaf and Avocado Salad*

---

*Peppered Poussins with Lime and
Sage Crumbs*
*Pasta with Rocket and Goat's Cheese*
*Bittersweet Roots*
*Seasonal Green Vegetable*
*Aubergines with Parsley*

---

*Fresh Ginger Cups*

SERVES 6

---

Our supper menu is easy to prepare. A colourful salad of mixed leaves and avocado is followed by poussins, which make a stunning centre-piece served with pasta, green vegetables, aubergine and jicama – a delicious root vegetable, not yet available here. Its flavour and texture are between parsnip and white radish (mooli), so we've tested our Bittersweet Roots with both. Finish with Fresh Ginger Cups.

---

### COUNTDOWN

**The day before**

Prepare the salad leaves for the starter and refrigerate in polythene bags. Fry the croûtons, drain, cover and store in a cool place. Make the salad dressing and store, covered. Prepare the poussins and marinate in the fridge overnight.

**On the day**
**To serve at 8 pm**

**About 5 pm:** Make the Fresh Ginger Cups but do not decorate. Chill. Prepare seasonal green vegetables, if serving. Fry the aubergines, drain thoroughly and layer in a serving dish. Cool.

**7.30 pm:** Cook the poussins and Bittersweet Roots. Keep the roots warm, covered, in a low oven. Reheat the aubergines in the oven.

**7.50 pm:** Put the seasonal green vegetables on to cook. Decorate the Fresh Ginger Cups.

**7.55 pm:** Put the water on for the pasta.

**8 pm:** Finish the salad and serve the meal.

# Mixed Leaf and Avocado Salad

*Choose a wide variety of colours and flavours for the salad leaves.*

mixed salad leaves
3 slices white or brown bread
oil
1 avocado

FOR THE DRESSING
60 ml (4 tbsp) olive oil
about 15 ml (1 tbsp) lemon juice
salt and pepper
5 ml (1 level tsp) French mustard, such as Dijon
1 garlic clove, skinned and crushed (optional)

1 Rinse, drain and dry the mixed salad leaves. Shred into rough-shaped pieces, then refrigerate in polythene bags.
2 Cut each slice of bread into small cubes and fry in hot oil until golden brown. Drain well on absorbent kitchen paper. Whisk together all of the dressing ingredients, including the garlic, if using.
3 Just before serving, halve the avocado and remove the stone. Peel and slice the flesh. Toss together the salad leaves, avocado and dressing. Scatter over the croûtons.

*315 Calories per serving*

# Peppered Poussins with Lime and Sage Crumbs

*If time allows, place the poussins with the oil and lime mixture in a non-metallic dish, cover and marinate in the fridge overnight.*

3 limes
1 whole bulb garlic
3 poussins
15 ml (1 level tbsp) coarsely ground black peppercorns
salt
75 ml (5 tbsp) olive oil
1 bunch spring onions, roughly chopped
30 ml (2 level tbsp) chopped fresh sage
50–75 g (2–3 oz) butter
175 g (6 oz) fresh wholemeal breadcrumbs
fresh sage leaves, to garnish

1 Thinly slice one lime. Grate the rind and squeeze the juice from the remaining two. Halve the bulb of garlic horizontally. Halve the poussins, discarding the backbones.
2 Mix together the lime slices, juice, peppercorns, salt and olive oil in a large, shallow, flameproof dish. Add the poussins and baste.
3 Cook the poussins under a hot grill, or on a barbecue, basting with the oil and lime mixture as they cook. Allow about 15 minutes on each side; the juices should run clear.
4 Meanwhile, place the spring onions, garlic, sage and lime rind in a large sauté pan with the butter. Sauté over a high heat for 2–3 minutes, then stir in the crumbs. Continue to cook, stirring, for 3–4 minutes or until golden and crisp. Discard the garlic.
5 Serve the grilled poussins on a bed of sautéed crumbs. Garnish with fresh sage leaves.

*455 Calories per serving*

# *P*ASTA WITH ROCKET AND GOAT'S CHEESE

*The heat of the freshly cooked pasta wilts the rocket and melts the goat's cheese mixture to form a sauce.*

350 g (12 oz) fresh or dried pasta shapes
salt and pepper
25 g (1 oz) fresh soft goat's cheese
45 ml (3 tbsp) single cream
45 ml (3 level tbsp) roughly chopped rocket or watercress

1 Cook the pasta in boiling salted water for 3–4 minutes if using fresh, or for 7–10 minutes if dried.
2 Meanwhile, beat together the goat's cheese and cream. Drain the pasta, and toss in the rocket and cheese mixture. Season and serve immediately.

*225 Calories per serving*

# *B*ITTERSWEET ROOTS

*Jicama is a delicious bittersweet root vegetable that looks like a smooth, dark type of celeriac.*

900 g (2 lb) jicama, parsnip or white radish (mooli)
30 ml (2 tbsp) oil
150 ml (¼ pint) chicken stock
25 g (1 oz) butter
salt and pepper

1 Wash and peel the vegetable and cut into long, thin strips. Heat the oil in a large sauté pan and cook the strips, stirring continuously, for a few minutes or until beginning to brown and soften.

2 Add the stock, butter and seasoning. Bring to the boil, lower the heat and bubble gently for about 7 minutes or until all the liquid has evaporated and the vegetable strips are glazed and tender.

*160 Calories per serving*

# *A*UBERGINES WITH PARSLEY

700 g (1½ lb) aubergines, thickly sliced
salt and pepper
flour
olive oil
1 small garlic clove, skinned and crushed
chopped fresh parsley

1 Put the aubergines in a colander and sprinkle generously with salt. Leave for 30 minutes, then rinse and dry thoroughly. Toss in a little seasoned flour.
2 Heat some oil in a large frying pan. When hot, fry the aubergines, a few at a time, until brown and tender. Drain and keep hot in a serving dish. Add more oil to the pan as required.
3 When all the aubergine slices are cooked, pour off all but 15 ml (1 tbsp) pan drippings and add the garlic and parsley. Spoon over the aubergine, season with pepper and serve.

*125 Calories per serving*

# $F$RESH GINGER CUPS

*The quickest of recipes. Make sure the ginger is grated on a fine blade to produce a smooth pulp.*

25 g (1 oz) piece fresh root ginger, peeled and finely grated
300 ml (10 fl oz) Greek-style natural yogurt
300 ml (10 fl oz) soured cream
150 ml (5 fl oz) lemon curd
whipped cream, herb flowers and icing sugar, to decorate

**1** Whisk together all the ingredients until evenly blended.
**2** Spoon into individual cups or ramekins. Decorate with whipped cream, herb flowers and sifted icing sugar.

*230 Calories per serving*

*Left to right: Aubergines with Parsley (page 13), Bittersweet Roots (page 13), steamed Swiss chard, Peppered Poussins with Lime and Sage Crumbs (page 12), Pasta with Rocket and Goat's Cheese (page 13)*

# No-Fuss Midweek Supper

---

## Menu

*Tomato Cups with Lime and Chive Dressing or Flageolet and
Tomato Salad with Herby Dressing*

---

*Italian Braised Beef
Mixed Rice Pilaff
Spinach and Bacon Salad*

---

*Apricot and Orange Custards*

SERVES 6

---

If you are entertaining midweek with only a limited amount of time to prepare and cook before your guests arrive, informality is the keynote to success. This simple yet inspired menu allows you to entertain in informal style at lightning speed with minimum fuss.

A midweek supper party should unwind your guests no matter how frenetic a day they've had. With a little forethought and planning, it's easy to create a relaxed atmosphere within an hour or so of arriving home yourself. The secret lies in getting most of the preparation out of the way the night before. Leave everything ready before you go out in the morning – even the table can be set the night before and glasses put out for pre-dinner drinks. Once you're home, arrange nibbles around the room, draw the curtains, and set the music and the lighting low. Finish off any last-minute touches to the food, then allow yourself at least a little time to relax.

--- **COUNTDOWN** ---

**Two days before**

Cut up the beef, mix with the marinade ingredients, cover and refrigerate.

**The day before**

Prepare the Tomato Cups to the end of step 3 or prepare the Flageolet and Tomato Salad, keeping the dressing separate. Cover and refrigerate. Wash the salad leaves and refrigerate in a polythene bag. Make the salad dressing and refrigerate. Prepare the Italian Braised

Beef to the end of step 4, cool, cover and refrigerate. Halve or quarter the mushrooms, halve or quarter the artichoke hearts, cover and refrigerate. Prepare the Mixed Rice Pilaff to the end of step 3. Toast the pine nuts and store in an airtight container. Chop the parsley, cover and refrigerate. Make the Spinach and Bacon Salad to the end of step 3. Prepare the Apricot and Orange Custards to the end of step 3. Spoon the custard mixture into separate glasses but do not spoon over the apricot purée. Cover and refrigerate the purée separately.

**On the day**
**To serve at 8 pm**
**6.30 pm:** Take the casserole and rice out of the fridge.
**6.45 pm:** Preheat the oven to 190°C (375°F) mark 5.
**7 pm:** Put the casserole (covered) on the top shelf of the oven to reheat. Take the custards from the fridge and spoon over the apricot purée. Return to the fridge until ready to serve.
**7.20 pm:** Place the rice in the oven.
**7.30 pm:** Fill the tomato shells with the avocado mixture, garnish and keep covered until serving time. Alternatively, dress the Flageolet and Tomato Salad and arrange on individual plates on a bed of lettuce. Garnish and cover.
**7.50 pm:** Toss the spinach salad and complete as directed in the main recipe. Add the mushrooms, artichokes and olives to the casserole, and simmer as directed. Stir the toasted pine nuts, parsley and seasoning into the rice.
**8 pm:** Serve the meal.

---

**FREEZER NOTES**
*The casserole is the only dish that will freeze. Cool, pack and freeze at the end of step 4. To use, thaw overnight at cool room temperature. Reheat as directed in the Countdown, stirring in an extra 150 ml (¼ pint) stock before putting it in the oven.*

---

# $T$OMATO CUPS WITH LIME AND CHIVE DRESSING

6 medium tomatoes, skinned
1 large, ripe avocado
15–30 ml (1–2 level tbsp) mayonnaise
juice of 2 limes
salt and pepper
50 g (2 oz) green pepper, de-seeded and finely chopped
6 spring onions, finely chopped
120 ml (8 tbsp) olive oil
30 ml (2 level tbsp) snipped fresh chives
15 ml (1 level tbsp) caster sugar
chives and salad leaves, to garnish

1 Cut the rounded ends off the tomatoes and reserve. Level the stalk ends, if necessary. Using a serrated knife and a teaspoon, scoop out all the seeds and flesh, leaving the shells intact. Sieve the flesh and reserve the juices. Place the tomato shells upside-down on a plate lined with absorbent kitchen paper. Cover and refrigerate.
2 Halve the avocado and remove the stone. Peel and roughly chop the flesh.
3 Mix the mayonnaise with 30 ml (2 tbsp) lime juice and seasoning. Gently stir in the avocado, peppers and spring onions until evenly coated with mayonnaise. Adjust the seasoning. Cover tightly, pushing a piece of damp greaseproof paper right down on to the surface, and refrigerate.
4 For the dressing, whisk together the reserved tomato juice and 30 ml (2 tbsp) lime juice with the olive oil, snipped chives and caster sugar. Season to taste. Cover and refrigerate.
5 Just before serving, spoon the avocado mixture into the tomato shells, top with the tomato lids and garnish with chives and salad leaves. Spoon over just a little of the dressing to serve.

*255 Calories per serving*

# Flageolet and Tomato Salad with Herby Dressing

*This is even quicker and easier to make than the Tomato Cups. It looks pretty served on a bed of frisée lettuce leaves.*

75 g (3 oz) mange-touts, trimmed and halved
150 ml (¼ pint) olive oil
45 ml (3 tbsp) lemon juice
60 ml (4 tbsp) bottled lemon-flavoured mayonnaise
45 ml (3 level tbsp) mixed chopped fresh herbs (parsley, chervil, chives, marjoram, basil)
salt and pepper
397 g (14 oz) can green flageolet beans, drained
6 tomatoes, skinned and chopped
1 small onion, skinned and finely chopped
2 garlic cloves, skinned and finely chopped
frisée lettuce leaves, chopped chives and lemon twists, to serve

1  Blanch the mange-touts in boiling water for 1 minute. Drain and refresh in cold water, then drain again.
2  Put the olive oil, lemon juice, mayonnaise, herbs and seasoning in a bowl and whisk until thick.
3  Rinse the flageolet beans under cold running water. Drain and add to the dressing with the mange-touts, tomatoes, onion and garlic.
4  Toss well, cover and chill for 30 minutes. Serve on lettuce leaves, garnished with chives and lemon twists.

*430 Calories per serving*

*Left to right: Spinach and Bacon Salad (page 20), Italian Braised Beef (above), Mixed Rice Pilaff (page 20)*

# Italian Braised Beef

1.1 kg (2½ lb) braising steak
350 g (12 oz) onion, skinned and roughly chopped
2 large garlic cloves, skinned and thinly sliced
75 cl (1¼ pint) bottle Chianti
olive oil
30 ml (2 level tbsp) tomato purée
15 ml (1 tbsp) wine vinegar
salt and pepper
bunch fresh thyme or 10 ml (2 level tsp) dried thyme
50 g (2 oz) plain flour
300 ml (½ pint) stock
175 g (6 oz) brown cap or button mushrooms, halved or quartered
397 g (14 oz) can artichoke hearts, drained and halved or quartered
about 18 pitted black olives

1  Cut the beef into 4 cm (1½ inch) cubes, discarding any excess fat. Place the beef, onion and garlic in a glass bowl with the wine, 45 ml (3 tbsp) olive oil, the tomato purée, vinegar and seasoning. Add the fresh thyme, tied in a bundle, or sprinkle in the dried thyme. Stir, cover and marinate in the fridge for at least 24 hours.
2  Strain off the marinade and reserve. Heat about 60 ml (4 tbsp) olive oil in a large flameproof casserole. Brown the meat, about one quarter at a time, adding a little more oil if necessary. Remove all the meat from the casserole.
3  Stir the flour into the pan and cook for 1 minute. Pour in the marinade and stock and bring to the boil. Replace the meat.
4  Cover the casserole tightly, then cook in the oven at 170°C (325°F) mark 3 for about 2 hours.
5  Ten minutes before serving, stir the mushrooms and artichokes into the casserole with the olives. Simmer on the hob for about 5 minutes. Adjust the seasoning and serve.

*475 Calories per serving*

# MIXED RICE PILAFF

*Wild rice is expensive but just a small amount adds real flavour and texture to this pilaff. It can be found in most health food shops and leading supermarkets.*

350 g (12 oz) long-grain brown rice
50 g (2 oz) wild rice
salt and pepper
60 ml (4 tbsp) olive oil
50 g (2 oz) toasted pine nuts
chopped fresh parsley

1 Cook the brown and wild rice according to packet instructions, until tender.
2 Drain the rice and rinse it under the cold tap to remove excess starch. Leave to drain.
3 Stir the oil into the rice with plenty of seasoning. Spoon into an ovenproof dish and cover tightly with damp greaseproof paper and the lid. Refrigerate until required.
4 Reheat in the oven at 190°C (375°F) mark 5 for about 40 minutes or until piping hot. Stir in the toasted pine nuts with plenty of parsley, and adjust the seasoning before serving.

*365 Calories per serving*

# SPINACH AND BACON SALAD

350 g (12 oz) fresh young spinach
175 g (6 oz) streaky bacon, de-rinded
45 ml (3 tbsp) olive oil
15 ml (1 tbsp) wine vinegar
5 ml (1 level tsp) Dijon mustard
salt and pepper

1 Pull any coarse stalks off the spinach and discard. Rinse the spinach in cold water. Drain well, pat dry and tear into bite-sized pieces. Refrigerate in a polythene bag.
2 Meanwhile, grill the bacon, drain on absorbent kitchen paper to remove excess fat, then snip into small pieces. Store, covered, in the fridge.
3 Whisk together the oil, vinegar, mustard and seasoning. Cover and set to one side.
4 When required, empty the spinach into a serving dish, toss with the dressing and scatter over the bacon bits.

*185 Calories per serving*

# APRICOT AND ORANGE CUSTARDS

*These light custards make the perfect ending to this supper menu. We liked their tangy flavour, but add a little sugar if you find apricots too sharp.*

454 g (16 oz) carton natural fromage frais
500 g (17.6 oz) carton fresh custard sauce
finely grated rind and juice of 2 oranges
400 g (14 oz) can apricots in natural juice, drained
caster sugar, to taste (optional)
sweet biscuits and single cream, to serve

1 Whisk together the fromage frais and the custard sauce until blended.
2 Stir the orange rind into the custard mixture with 60 ml (4 tbsp) strained orange juice. Mix thoroughly.
3 Place the apricots in a food processor and blend until quite smooth. Add caster sugar to taste, if using.
4 Spoon the custard into six tall, stemmed glasses and top each with the apricot purée. Serve accompanied by sweet, crisp biscuits and single cream.

*265 Calories per serving*

# $P$REPARE-AHEAD SUPPER

---

## Menu

*Sesame Cheese Pastries*

---

*Honeyed Lamb with Spiced Fruit*
*Steamed Couscous and Watercress*
*Peppered Vegetables*
*Buttered Greens*

---

*Chocolate and Chestnut Cream Vacherin*

SERVES 6

---

We all know that the best dishes for entertaining are those that require little last-minute attention, and they're better still if they can be prepared in advance and frozen. So here is the ideal menu.

The pastries are very simple, using ready-made hummus, and can be made ahead and stored in the fridge or freezer, ready to cook. The casserole is a delicious mix of lamb, subtly flavoured with honey and spices. It also freezes well, or it will keep in the fridge for a day or two. Lightly spiced prunes and pears are stirred in just before serving. The dessert is a variation on a classic recipe that chocolate lovers will adore. Again, it's made ahead.

--- COUNTDOWN ---

**One or two days before**
Make the sesame dressing for the Sesame Cheese Pastries. Make the Honeyed Lamb to the end of step 3, then cool and refrigerate. Make the Spiced Fruit to the end of step 2. Make the meringue rounds and store in an airtight tin.

**One day before**
Make the Sesame Cheese Pastries to the end of step 3, then refrigerate. Prepare the Steamed Couscous and Watercress to the end of step 1, cover and refrigerate. Prepare the Peppered Vegetables to the end of step 1, cool and store

in the refrigerator. Prepare 900 g (2 lb) spring greens, if using. Refrigerate in a polythene bag. Make the filling for the vacherin and store in the refrigerator.

**On the day**

**To serve at 8 pm**

**6 pm:** Wash the salad garnish for the Sesame Cheese Pastries. Arrange on individual serving plates and refrigerate. Spoon the couscous mixture into a colander lined with muslin or a blue J-cloth, and place over a pan of water, ready to steam. Chop the watercress, cover and set aside.

**6.45 pm:** Preheat the oven to 190°C (375°F) mark 5. Finish the vacherin.

**7 pm:** Add the lemon juice, oil and seasoning to the Peppered Vegetables and put them in the oven to cook. Bring the Honeyed Lamb to the boil, cover and leave to simmer gently.

**7.30 pm:** Put the Sesame Cheese Pastries in the oven. Stir the Peppered Vegetables. Steam the couscous.

**7.45 pm:** Slice the pears into the spiced prunes.

**8 pm:** Strain the Spiced Fruit and stir into the Honeyed Lamb. Leave over a very gentle heat. Put the spring greens on to steam or boil, if serving. Serve the starter.

---

### FREEZER NOTES

*Freeze the Sesame Cheese Pastries at the end of step 3. To use, cook from frozen in the oven at 190°C (375°F) mark 5 for 30 minutes. Cool, pack and freeze the Honeyed Lamb at the end of step 3. Freeze the couscous at the end of step 1. Freeze the Peppered Vegetables at the end of step 1. Thaw all three dishes overnight at cool room temperature. The meringue rounds can be frozen but store well in an airtight tin.*

---

*Left to right: Steamed Couscous and Watercress (page 25), Honeyed Lamb with Spiced Fruit (pages 24–5), buttered greens, Peppered Vegetables (page 26)*

# Sesame Cheese Pastries

*These crisp pastries are filled with a delicious mixture of ready-made hummus with low-fat soft cheese and a little extra garlic. They're the ideal starter or savoury to serve with drinks, as they can be made ahead and cooked from frozen. If you're not running to time, the pastries will keep warm and crisp, uncovered, in a low oven for an extra 10–15 minutes.*

125 g (4 oz) hummus
175 g (6 oz) low-fat soft cheese
1 garlic clove, skinned and crushed
salt and pepper
6 sheets filo pastry, each measuring about 51×25 cm (20×10 inches)
50 g (2 oz) butter, melted
sesame seeds
150 ml (¼ pint) olive oil
30 ml (2 tbsp) white wine vinegar
crispy fried aubergine slices, or salad leaves, to garnish

1 Beat together the hummus, soft cheese, garlic and pepper.
2 Cut each filo pastry sheet into four squares, each about 12.5 cm (5 inches). There should be 24 in total.
3 Brush one square lightly with melted butter. Spoon a little of the hummus mixture into the centre and fold the pastry over to enclose it, like a parcel. Butter another square of pastry, place the hummus parcel in the centre and fold up to enclose as before. (This double layer helps to stop the parcels from bursting while cooking.) Brush lightly all over with butter, sprinkle with sesame seeds and place on a baking sheet. Repeat until all the filling and pastry is used. Chill the pastries for 20 minutes.
4 Whisk together the oil and vinegar with some toasted sesame seeds to make a dressing. Season. Cook the pastries in the oven at 190°C (375°F) mark 5 for 25–30 minutes or until golden brown and crisp. Serve the pastries with a little dressing drizzled over, garnished with crispy fried aubergine slices or salad leaves.

*350 Calories per serving*

# Honeyed Lamb

*Start this recipe a day or two before it's required so the flavours develop, then all that's needed is a final 20 minutes' simmering before you serve it.*

1.4 kg (3 lb) boned leg of lamb
oil
175 g (6 oz) onions, skinned and roughly chopped
1 garlic clove, skinned and crushed
10 ml (2 level tsp) ground allspice
a pinch of ground chilli
1 cinnamon stick
50 g (2 oz) plain flour
30 ml (2 level tbsp) honey
30 ml (2 level tbsp) tomato purée
salt and pepper
1 litre (1¾ pints) stock
pared rind and strained juice of 2 oranges
pared rind and strained juice of 1 lemon
1 quantity Spiced Fruit (see right)

1 Cube the lamb, discarding any fat. Heat 45 ml (3 tbsp) oil in a flameproof casserole. Brown the lamb, a few pieces at a time, adding more oil if necessary. Drain well.
2 Add the onions to the casserole and cook, stirring, over a low heat until softened. Stir in the garlic and spices. Cook, stirring, for 1 minute before adding the flour, honey, tomato purée and seasoning. Stir in the stock, lamb and rind and juice of the oranges and lemon. Bring to the boil.

3 Cover the casserole tightly and cook in the oven at 170°C (325°F) mark 3 for 1 hour. Remove from the oven, cool and refrigerate.

4 When ready to use, skim off any excess fat. Bring slowly to the boil, cover and simmer for a further 20 minutes or until the lamb is very tender. Stir in the strained Spiced Fruit. Adjust the seasoning and serve.

*680 Calories per serving*

---

# SPICED FRUIT

*These sweet/sour fruit are delicious stirred into the lamb casserole, or try them with hot or cold roast pork.*

300 ml (½ pint) distilled malt vinegar
1 clove
175 g (6 oz) granulated sugar
2.5 cm (1 inch) piece of fresh root ginger, peeled and grated
12 prunes
4 firm pears

1 Place the vinegar, clove, sugar and ginger in a small saucepan. Heat gently until the sugar has completely dissolved, then leave to cool.

2 Place the prunes in a large bowl and strain over the spiced vinegar. Cover closely with cling film and leave to soak for one or two nights.

3 About 15 minutes before required, halve, core and thickly slice the pears into the vinegar. Strain before use.

*40 Calories per serving*

---

# STEAMED COUSCOUS AND WATERCRESS

175 g (6 oz) couscous
25 g (1 oz) brown rice, cooked
75 g (3 oz) butter, melted
salt and pepper
1 bunch watercress, chopped

1 Cover the couscous with 300 ml (½ pint) cold water. Leave for 10 minutes or until all the water is absorbed. Add the rice, melted butter and seasoning, forking out any lumps.

2 Spoon the couscous mixture into a wire sieve or metal colander lined with muslin or a blue J-cloth. Set over a pan of boiling water and cover with foil. Leave to steam for about 35 minutes.

3 Stir in the watercress. Adjust the seasoning and serve.

*165 Calories per serving*

---

# Peppered Vegetables

700 g (1½ lb) parsnips
700 g (1½ lb) carrots
salt and pepper
juice of 1 large lemon, strained
75 ml (5 tbsp) olive oil

1 Peel and cut the parsnips and carrots into long, thick sticks. Cover with cold, salted water and bring to the boil. Boil for 2–3 minutes. Drain well.
2 Spoon the parsnips and carrots into a large roasting tin. Stir in the strained lemon juice, olive oil, salt and plenty of pepper.
3 Cook, uncovered, in the oven at 190°C (375°F) mark 5 for 1 hour or until tender and golden. Stir once during cooking.

*160 Calories per serving*

# Chocolate and Chestnut Cream Vacherin

*Layers of hazelnut meringue are sandwiched together with a delicious mixture of chestnut purée, melted chocolate and cream.*

6 egg whites
350 g (12 oz) caster sugar
75 g (3 oz) hazelnuts, skinned, toasted and finely chopped
175 g (6 oz) plain chocolate, broken into pieces
500 g (1.1 lb) can sweetened chestnut purée
284 ml (10 fl oz) carton double cream
whipped cream and cocoa powder, to decorate

1 Line three baking sheets with non-stick baking parchment and draw a 20.5 cm (8 inch) circle on each.
2 Stiffly whisk the egg whites, then gradually whisk in the sugar, a little at a time, whisking well until the meringue is smooth and shiny. Very lightly fold in the hazelnuts.
3 Either spread the mixture over the marked circles, or transfer to a piping bag fitted with a 1 cm (½ inch) plain nozzle and pipe the meringue in a spiral over the marked circles, starting from the centre.
4 Bake in the oven at 140°C (275°F) mark 1 for 1–1½ hours or until dried out. Change the positions of the baking sheets during cooking so that the meringues dry out evenly. Remove from the oven and leave to cool, then carefully remove the lining papers. Store in airtight containers until required.
5 Melt the chocolate in a heatproof bowl set over a pan of simmering water. Put the chestnut purée in a bowl and beat until softened. Stir in the melted chocolate. Lightly whip the cream until soft peaks form, and fold it into the chestnut mixture.
6 To assemble the vacherin, sandwich the meringues together with a little of the chestnut cream. Cover the top and sides with the remainder and decorate with whipped cream and cocoa powder.

*865 Calories per serving*

# *L*OW-FAT
# FEAST

## *Menu*

*Steamed Mussels in Pepper Broth* or
*Smoked Mackerel Mousse*

---

*Pork Tenderloin with Orange and Ginger*
*Creamed Garlic Potatoes*
*Shredded Cabbage*

---

*Apple Mint Meringues*

SERVES 6

Dieting and dinner parties are not usually synonymous. Yet, with a little imagination, it is possible to entertain *and* count calories without putting your guests through an endurance test of dull food. By choosing ingredients carefully and making use of the low-fat and low-sugar products available, we show you how to entertain in grand style on about 750 calories (or 840 with two glasses of wine) – and your guests need never know.

Mussels make an excellent starter – rich in protein and vitamins, yet low in fat and calories. Alternatively, why not try Smoked Mackerel Mousse? Lean white meat is always the best choice for a main dish. We've opted for pork tenderloins, reasonably priced and quick to cook, in a citrus sauce spiked with ginger.

## —— COUNTDOWN ——

**The day before**
Make the Smoked Mackerel Mousse if serving instead of the mussels. Make the pepper broth for the mussels, if serving, by following step 2. Cool, cover and refrigerate in a bowl. Place the pork tenderloins in the ginger and citrus marinade. Cover and refrigerate. Prepare the carrots. Shred the cabbage. Refrigerate separately in polythene bags. Make the meringues. Allow to cool and store in an airtight container. Cook the apple slices, cool, cover and refrigerate.

**On the day**
Prepare the mussels and refrigerate. Cook and sieve the potatoes. Cool, cover and refrigerate.

27

**To serve at 8 pm**

**6.30 pm:** Brown and cook the tenderloins. Remove to a chopping board but don't slice yet. Cover loosely with foil. Boil and reduce the pan juices, then set to one side.

**7 pm:** Assemble the Apple Mint Meringues and refrigerate. Drain the mussels, then put them into a saucepan with the water and a bay leaf.

**7.30 pm:** Put the pepper broth in a saucepan ready to reheat. Place the potatoes in a saucepan with the yogurt or cream and the seasoning, ready to reheat. Put a pan of water on to boil for the cabbage. Slice the pork tenderloins and add to the ginger sauce with the half-fat butter spread.

**7.40 pm:** Cook the shredded cabbage and toss with the half-fat butter spread. Reheat the creamed potatoes. Keep both warm, covered, in ovenproof dishes in a low oven.

**7.50 pm:** Steam the mussels and reheat the pepper broth. Strain the cooking liquid from the mussels into the broth and add the dill. Bring the pork and sauce to the boil, cover and simmer *very gently* while serving the mussels or mackerel mousse.

---

### FREEZER NOTES
*Only the pepper broth for the mussels is suitable for freezing. Thaw overnight at cool room temperature.*

---

# Steamed mussels in pepper broth

*Always buy more mussels than you need as a few will be discarded before and after cooking. Allow about 350 g (12 oz) per person for a starter and 450 g (1 lb) for a main course.*

2 kg (4½ lb) fresh mussels in their shells
15 ml (1 tbsp) olive oil
175 g (6 oz) onion, skinned and finely chopped
225 g (8 oz) red pepper, de-seeded and finely chopped
2 bay leaves
1 garlic clove, skinned and crushed
450 g (1 lb) tomatoes, skinned, de-seeded and finely chopped
45 ml (3 level tbsp) chopped fresh dill
diced red pepper, to garnish

1  Discard any cracked mussels and any that remain open when tapped smartly on the shell. Scrub the mussels and pull off the coarse threads (beards) from the side of the shells.

2  Heat the oil in a medium saucepan. Sauté the onion with the red pepper, 1 bay leaf and the garlic until it begins to soften. Add the tomatoes and cook, stirring, for 1–2 minutes before adding 600 ml (1 pint) water. Bring to the boil, then reduce the heat, cover and simmer for about 15 minutes. Purée the mixture in a blender or food processor, then sieve into a clean saucepan. Season.

3  Place the mussels in one large saucepan. Add 150 ml (¼ pint) water and the remaining bay leaf. Cover the pan tightly and place over a high heat. Steam the mussels, shaking the pan occasionally, for 3–5 minutes. Afterwards, discard any mussels that have not opened.

4  Strain the cooking liquid from the mussels into the pepper broth. Stir in the chopped dill and bring to the boil. Adjust the seasoning. Divide the mussels among six individual serving bowls and pour over the pepper broth. Garnish with diced red pepper.

5  To eat, use an empty shell like a pair of tweezers to pinch the mussels from their shells. Set a plate beside each guest for the 'empties'. You will also need spoons for the pepper broth.

*145 Calories per serving*

# SMOKED MACKEREL MOUSSE

300 ml (½ pint) milk
a few slices of onion and carrot
1 bay leaf
25 g (1 oz) half-fat butter spread
30 ml (2 level tbsp) plain flour
10 ml (2 level tsp) powdered gelatine
275 g (10 oz) smoked mackerel fillet
50 g (2 oz) onion, skinned and chopped
15 ml (1 level tbsp) creamed horseradish
150 ml (¼ pint) natural yogurt
15 ml (1 tbsp) lemon juice
salt and pepper
2 egg whites

1 Pour the milk into a saucepan, add the flavourings and bring slowly to the boil. Remove from the heat, cover and leave to infuse for 30 minutes.

2 Strain the milk into a jug. Melt the spread in the rinsed-out pan, add the flour and cook gently, stirring, for 1–2 minutes. Remove from the heat and gradually blend in the milk. Bring to the boil, stirring, then simmer for 3 minutes or until thick and smooth. Remove from the heat and sprinkle in the gelatine. Stir until dissolved. Cool for 20 minutes.

3 Meanwhile, flake the smoked mackerel fillet, discarding the skin and bones.

4 Work the cooled sauce, mackerel, onion and horseradish in a blender or food processor until smooth. Pour into a bowl and stir in the yogurt, lemon juice and salt and pepper.

5 Whisk the egg whites until they stand in soft peaks, then fold gently into the fish mixture.

6 Spoon the mousse into six individual dishes and chill in the refrigerator for at least 2 hours or until set. Serve chilled.

*205 Calories per serving*

# PORK TENDERLOIN WITH ORANGE AND GINGER

grated rind and juice of 1 orange
grated rind and juice of 1 lemon
50 g (2 oz) piece of fresh root ginger, peeled and finely grated or chopped
15 ml (1 level tbsp) Hoisin sauce
15 ml (1 level tbsp) artificial granulated sweetener
1 garlic clove, skinned and crushed
2 pork tenderloins, about 700 g (1 ½ lb) total weight
225 g (8 oz) carrots, peeled
oil
300 ml (½ pint) chicken stock
50 g (2 oz) half-fat butter spread
salt and pepper

1 Stir together the grated rinds and 50 ml (2 fl oz) each of orange and lemon juice. Add the ginger, Hoisin sauce, sweetener and garlic.

2 Trim the tenderloins of any excess fat. Place in a large, shallow dish. Pour over the ginger mixture, cover and marinate in the fridge for 3–4 hours, preferably overnight.

3 Cut the carrots into 5 cm (2 inch) matchstick lengths. Drain the pork from the marinade. Lightly grease a large non-stick frying pan with a little oil. Brown the pork tenderloins well on all sides. Pour over the ginger marinade and the chicken stock, and add the carrots. Cover and simmer very gently for about 15 minutes or until the pork and the carrots are cooked.

4 Remove the tenderloins with a slotted spoon and slice thickly. Boil the pan juices for 2–3 minutes to reduce by about half or until slightly thickened and syrupy. Off the heat, gradually whisk the spread into the sauce. Season.

5 Return the pork to the pan, cover and simmer very gently for 1–2 minutes or until heated through.

*230 Calories per serving*

# CREAMED GARLIC POTATOES

1.4 kg (3 lb) old potatoes, peeled and roughly chopped
salt and pepper
1 garlic clove, skinned and crushed
45 ml (3 tbsp) Greek-style natural yogurt or 30 ml (2 tbsp) single cream
grated nutmeg, to serve

1 Cook the potatoes in boiling salted water for 15–20 minutes or until very tender. Drain well. Sieve or press through a potato ricer until very smooth.
2 Beat in the garlic and the yogurt or cream. Adjust the seasoning and reheat gently before serving sprinkled with the grated nutmeg.

*185 Calories per serving*

———————— ༅ ————————

# SHREDDED CABBAGE

700 g (1½ lb) savoy cabbage
salt and pepper
25 g (1 oz) half-fat butter spread

1 Finely shred the cabbage, discarding the core and any coarse outer leaves.
2 Cook in boiling salted water for a few minutes only, until just tender.
3 Drain well. Toss with the half-fat butter spread. Adjust the seasoning.

*50 Calories per serving*

———————— ༅ ————————

# APPLE MINT MERINGUES

2 egg whites
125 g (4 oz) caster sugar
350 g (12 oz) tart eating apples, peeled, cored and thinly sliced
15 ml (1 level tbsp) granulated artificial sweetener
4 fresh mint sprigs
150 g (5 oz) Greek-style natural yogurt
15 ml (1 level tbsp) icing sugar, sprigs of fresh mint and apple slices, to decorate

1 Whisk the egg whites until stiff but not dry. Add 30 ml (2 level tbsp) caster sugar and whisk again until stiff and shiny. Fold in the remaining sugar.
2 Mark twelve 7.5 cm (3 inch) rounds on a sheet of non-stick baking parchment. Divide the meringue mixture among the rounds and spread with a round-bladed knife to fill. Alternatively, using a 0.5 cm (¼ inch) plain nozzle, pipe the mixture into the rounds. Bake in the oven at 140°C (275°F) mark 1 for about 1 hour or until completely dried out and crisp. Leave to cool on a wire rack.
3 Place the apples in a saucepan with the artificial sweetener, four sprigs of mint and 30 ml (2 tbsp) water. Cover and cook very gently for about 10 minutes or until the apple has softened. Cool, cover and chill for at least 1 hour. Discard the mint.
4 To serve, spoon a little apple on to six meringue rounds. Top with the yogurt and the remaining meringues. Dust lightly with icing sugar and decorate with sprigs of fresh mint and apple slices.

*135 Calories per serving*

———————— ༅ ————————

*Steamed Mussels in Pepper Broth (page 28)*

# DIETING IN STYLE

## Menu

### Watercress Soup

---

### Mixed-Pepper Poussins
### Grilled Chicory
### Seasonal Vegetables
### New Potatoes

---

### Vanilla Poached Pears
### Caramel Lattices
### Cinnamon Crisps

SERVES 6

---

This menu is specially designed for those on a low-fat diet, either to reduce high cholesterol levels, or as part of a healthy weight-loss programme.

The standard fare of grilled fish or chicken with boiled vegetables is predictable, but as this menu shows, low-fat meals needn't be anything but delicious. Our delicately flavoured Watercress Soup makes an elegant start to the meal. Try serving it with a swirl of Greek-style yogurt on top of each portion.

Although red meat is not forbidden on low-fat diets, white meat, like chicken and turkey, contains less fat. Poussins, or spring chickens, are perfect for entertaining and full of flavour. We've stuffed them with a mixture of red and yellow peppers and sun-dried tomatoes, which makes the dish colourful.

Make the most of seasonal vegetables. You can eat as many as you like, as long as you don't add butter. We served asparagus, patty pan squash and sugar snap peas, along with grilled chicory and new potatoes.

The Vanilla Poached Pears make a light and refreshing finale, decorated with Caramel Lattices and accompanied by Cinnamon Crisps.

32

## —— COUNTDOWN ——

### The week before

Order poussins from your butcher. Make and freeze the sorbet. Make the Cinnamon Crisps to the end of step 5 and store in an airtight container.

### The day before

Make the Watercress Soup. Purée and store in the fridge. Make the stock from the poussin bones. Cool, cover and refrigerate. Prepare the stuffing, cover and store in the fridge. Prepare the Vanilla Poached Pears to the end of step 3. Make the Caramel Lattices and store in an airtight container.

### On the day

In the morning, stuff the poussins and place in the fridge. Top and tail the sugar snap peas, trim the asparagus, cover and refrigerate. Slice the squash, cover and refrigerate in water (with a few drops of lemon juice). Scrub 900 g (2 lb) new potatoes.

### To serve at 8 pm

**3.30 pm:** Make the caramel for the Cinnamon Crisps, decorate the biscuits and store in an airtight container.

**6.20 pm:** Preheat the oven to 200°C (400°F) mark 6.

**6.50 pm:** Place the poussins in the oven to cook.

**7.20 pm:** Cook the potatoes.

**7.35 pm:** Remove the poussins from the oven. Cut in half ready to serve, then transfer to an ovenproof serving dish, cover with foil and keep warm in a low oven. Gently boil the juices. Before serving, whisk in the fromage frais and the chopped parsley. Drain the potatoes, transfer to an ovenproof dish and keep warm.

**7.45 pm:** Cook the asparagus, patty pan squash and sugar snap peas. Blanch, halve and grill the chicory. Transfer to heatproof serving dishes and keep warm in the oven. Reheat the soup.

**8 pm:** Serve the meal. Decorate the Vanilla Poached Pears just before serving.

# WATERCRESS SOUP

15 g (½ oz) butter or margarine
1 medium onion, skinned and chopped
2 large bunches watercress, trimmed and roughly chopped
40 g (1½ oz) plain flour
600 ml (1 pint) chicken or vegetable stock, skimmed
600 ml (1 pint) semi-skimmed milk
grated nutmeg
salt and pepper
watercress sprigs and paprika, to garnish

1  Melt the butter in a heavy-based saucepan. Add the onion and watercress, cover and cook over a low heat for 3–5 minutes or until the onion is soft but not brown, shaking the pan occasionally.

2  Add the flour and cook for 1 minute, then gradually stir in the stock, milk and nutmeg to taste. Bring to the boil, stirring. Season with salt and pepper, lower the heat and simmer, covered, for about 15 minutes or until thickened and smooth.

3  Remove from the heat and leave to cool slightly, then purée in a blender or food processor. Return the soup to the saucepan and reheat. Serve in individual bowls, garnished with watercress sprigs and a sprinkling of paprika.

*100 Calories per serving*

# MIXED-PEPPER POUSSINS

*Your butcher should be happy to bone the poussins for you, provided you give enough notice. We've allowed four poussins (eight portions) for six people, which leaves two halves for second helpings. Ask the butcher for the bones to make some chicken stock to use in the recipe. We contacted several butchers around the country who were all willing to bone the poussins, but if you can't buy them boned, stuff whole birds.*

2 red peppers, about 175 g (6 oz) each
3 yellow peppers, about 175 g (6 oz) each
1 bunch spring onions
3 celery sticks
75 g (3 oz) sun-dried tomatoes in oil
125 g (4 oz) wholemeal breadcrumbs
salt and pepper
4 boned poussins, about 250 g (9 oz) each
300 ml (½ pint) dry white wine
300 ml (½ pint) chicken stock
1 garlic clove, skinned and crushed
30 ml (2 level tbsp) fromage frais
30 ml (2 level tbsp) chopped fresh parsley
flat-leaf parsley, to garnish

1 Cut the peppers in half and place, skin-side up, on a large baking sheet. (There is no need to remove the stalks or seeds at this stage.) Place under a hot grill for about 15 minutes or until the skin becomes black and charred. Cover the peppers with a damp tea-towel and set aside until cool.

2 Chop the spring onions and celery. Drain the tomatoes of most of their oil and chop the flesh into small pieces. Reserve the oil.

3 When the peppers are cool, rub the skins off under a running tap. Discard the seeds and stalks, then chop the remaining flesh into long, thin strips.

4 Place the peppers, spring onions, celery and sun-dried tomatoes in a frying pan and gently sauté for about 10 minutes or until tender. Add a little of the reserved oil, if necessary. Add the breadcrumbs and mix well. Season with salt and pepper.

5 Place the boned poussins, breast-side down, on a flat surface. If they are not already split open (many butchers cleverly bone birds without cutting them open), cut them horizontally through the skin along the line of what would have been the backbone.

6 Scrape a little of the flesh away from the sides towards the middle and trim away any excess skin. Place a quarter of the stuffing inside each bird. Bring the sides together to enclose the stuffing and secure with cocktail sticks, or sew with fine string. Turn the poussins over and plump back into shape. (Cook any remaining stuffing separately in an ovenproof dish.)

7 Put the birds in a roasting tin just large enough to hold them without squashing them together. Add the wine, stock and garlic. Bring to the boil on the hob.

8 Transfer to the oven and cook at 200°C (400°F) mark 6 for 45–50 minutes or until the juices run clear when you insert a skewer.

9 When the birds are cooked, cut them in half lengthways with a sharp knife or scissors and transfer from the roasting tin to an ovenproof serving dish. Cover and keep warm in the oven. Transfer the juices to a saucepan and boil until reduced by one third. Season with salt and pepper. Just before serving, whisk in the fromage frais and chopped parsley (take care not to boil or it may curdle). Garnish with flat-leaf parsley. Serve with seasonal vegetables, grilled chicory and new potatoes.

*350 Calories per serving*

*Mixed Pepper Poussins (above), Grilled Chicory, Seasonal Vegetables (page 36), new potatoes*

# GRILLED CHICORY

8 small heads chicory, about 550 g (1¼ lb) total weight
salt
30 ml (2 tbsp) oil

1 Cut the chicory in half lengthways. Place in a saucepan of boiling salted water and boil for 1 minute. Drain well and pat dry with absorbent kitchen paper.
2 Place on a grill rack and brush lightly with a little oil. Cook under a preheated grill for 3–4 minutes each side or until golden brown.

*10 Calories per serving*

# SEASONAL VEGETABLES

*We enjoyed a mixture of crisp vegetables with the poussins.*

225 g (8 oz) sugar snap peas
225 g (8 oz) asparagus
225 g (8 oz) patty pan squash
salt and pepper

1 Top and tail the sugar snap peas. Trim the asparagus into 7.5 cm (3 inch) lengths and thickly slice the patty pan squash.
2 Place the vegetables in a large saucepan of boiling salted water and simmer for 7–10 minutes or until tender. Drain.
3 Season with pepper before serving.

*25 Calories per serving*

# VANILLA POACHED PEARS

*You'll find vanilla pods in jars on the spice shelves in major supermarkets. If you can't obtain any, simply add a few more drops of vanilla essence in step 1.*

200 ml (7 fl oz) dry white wine
45 ml (3 tbsp) lemon juice
50 g (2 oz) caster sugar
1 vanilla pod, split, plus a few drops of vanilla essence
6 firm but ripe pears, about 800–900 g (1¾–2 lb) total weight
fresh bay leaves (optional) and Caramel Lattices, to decorate
crème fraîche or soured cream, to serve

1 Place the wine, lemon juice, caster sugar and vanilla pod together with a few drops of vanilla essence in a large saucepan with 450 ml (¾ pint) water. Stir gently over a low heat until all the sugar has dissolved.
2 Peel and halve the pears, but don't core them. Add to the wine mixture. Bring to the boil, then simmer, covered, for 12–15 minutes or until the pears look slightly translucent but are still firm.
3 Using draining spoons, lift the pears out of the pan and place them in a bowl. Bubble down the juices to reduce slightly. Add a little more vanilla essence if wished. Strain the syrup over the pears, cool, cover and chill until needed.
4 Serve one pear half per person on individual plates with a little syrup spooned over. Top, if wished, with a fresh bay leaf and Caramel Lattices. Serve with crème fraîche. Place the remaining pears in a serving dish to offer as second helpings.

*100 Calories per serving (whole pear)*

# CARAMEL LATTICES

*It's important to work quickly or the caramel will set in the pan. The lattices are brittle, so ease off the spoons gently.*

oil
75 g (3 oz) granulated sugar

1 Oil the backs of six stainless-steel table or dessertspoons. Place them on a wire rack over an oiled baking sheet.
2 Place the sugar in a small, heavy-based saucepan with 45 ml (3 tbsp) water. Dissolve over a gentle heat, stirring occasionally. Increase the heat and bubble to a caramel.
3 Immediately take the pan off the heat and quickly dip the base in and out of cold water, stirring all the time to prevent the caramel setting.
4 While the caramel is still liquid but beginning to thicken, drizzle it from the end of a dessertspoon, allowing it to run back and forth over the oiled spoons to create caramel lattices. Work quickly before the caramel sets.
5 Leave to harden, then gently ease off the spoons. Store in an airtight container (for not more than 3 days).

*50 Calories per lattice*

# CINNAMON CRISPS

50 g (2 oz) butter or margarine
2 egg whites
125 g (4 oz) caster sugar
50 g (2 oz) plain flour, sifted
2.5 ml (½ level tsp) ground cinnamon
75 g (3 oz) granulated sugar (optional)

1 Melt the butter in a saucepan and allow to cool, but don't leave it too long or it will solidify.
2 Whisk the egg whites until stiff but not dry, then fold in the caster sugar, melted butter, flour and cinnamon.
3 Spoon two heaped teaspoonfuls of mixture on to a greased baking sheet and spread each spoonful into a thin, almost transparent, 10 cm (4 inch) diameter circle.
4 Bake in the oven at 190°C (375°F) mark 5 for 5–6 minutes or until just tinged with colour and well browned around the edges. Immediately remove with a fish slice and wind the biscuits around the oiled handles of wooden spoons. Cool slightly, then gently ease off and place on a wire rack to cool. If the biscuits harden during shaping, return them to the oven briefly.
5 Continue baking in batches until all the mixture is used. Oil the baking sheet between batches, if necessary.
6 To decorate with caramel, place the biscuits well apart on a wire rack with an oiled baking sheet beneath. Not more than 5 hours before serving, place the granulated sugar in a saucepan and heat slowly until it melts. Increase the heat a little and continue until the sugar turns a deep caramel colour.
7 Using an oiled teaspoon or fork and working quickly, drizzle the caramel over the biscuits and leave to set.

MAKES ABOUT 12

*110 Calories per biscuit*

# *L*OW COST, HIGH STYLE

## *Menu*

*Filo Purses with Stir-Fried Vegetables*

*Chicken in Cider and Honey*
*Braised Baby Onions*
*Toasted Polenta*
*Peas with Leeks and Pancetta*

*Muscovado Creams* or *Coconut Crème Caramel*
*Tuiles*

SERVES 6

Counting the pennies doesn't mean short-changing your guests. This dinner has been put together with budgeting in mind, and shows that low-cost entertaining needn't be without style. The crisp Filo Purses and flavoursome Chicken in Cider and Honey are grand enough to grace any table, especially when served with our Italian-style vegetables. Your guests should find the Toasted Polenta a pleasant change from the usual potatoes or bread. For dessert, make one of our imaginative puddings to end the meal in style. The choice is between Muscovado Creams and Coconut Crème Caramel, both delicious served with crisp Tuiles biscuits.

## ——————— COUNTDOWN ———————

**The day before**

Prepare the Filo Purses to the end of step 4. Cover loosely and refrigerate. Complete the Chicken in Cider and Honey to the end of step 6, but don't fry the apple wedges yet. Cool quickly, cover and refrigerate. Slice the leeks and chop the pancetta. Refrigerate separately in polythene bags. Peel the onions and chop the parsley. Cover and keep at cool room temperature. Prepare the Polenta to the end of step 3. Keep covered in the fridge. Prepare the Muscovado Creams or the Coconut Crème Caramel and keep, covered, in the fridge. Make the Tuiles and store in an airtight container.

**On the day**

**To serve at 8 pm**

**About 6.30 pm:** Sauté the leeks with the pancetta to the end of step 1. Sauté the onions for Braised Baby Onions to the end of step 1. Place the Polenta on the grill pan ready to toast.

**About 7 pm:** Preheat the oven to 200°C (400°F) mark 6.

**7.30 pm:** Add the wine and parsley to the onions. Cover and simmer.

**7.40 pm:** Place the Filo Purses in the oven on the top shelf to cook. Bring the Chicken in Cider and Honey quickly to the boil, reduce the heat and simmer very gently for about 20 minutes or until heated through. Finish as directed. Grill the Polenta, cover and keep warm in the oven.

**7.50 pm:** Add the peas, stock and seasoning to the leek mixture. Cover and simmer for 3–4 minutes. Sauté the apple wedges to garnish the Chicken in Cider and Honey.

**8 pm:** Serve the Filo Purses. Turn the oven down to 100°C (200°F) mark low to keep the main course warm while you enjoy the starter.

---

### FREEZER NOTES

*Cool, pack and freeze the Chicken in Honey and Cider at the end of step 6. To use, thaw overnight at cool room temperature. Bring to the boil, adding more stock if necessary, cover and simmer in the oven at 200°C (400°F) mark 6 for 30 minutes, or on the hob for 15–20 minutes. The apple wedges are not suitable for freezing and must be prepared and sautéed when required.*

---

# $F$ILO PURSES WITH STIR-FRIED VEGETABLES

125 g (4 oz) celery
125 g (4 oz) carrots
75 g (3 oz) spring onions
butter or margarine
2.5 cm (1 inch) piece of fresh root ginger, peeled and finely chopped
125 g (4 oz) bean sprouts
juice of 1 small lemon, strained
salt and pepper
5 sheets filo pastry, each measuring about 45.5×30.5 cm (18×12 inches)
parsley sprigs, to garnish

1 Cut the celery, carrots and spring onions into thin shreds 5 cm (2 inches) long.

2 Heat 40 g (1½ oz) butter in a large sauté pan and add the ginger, shredded vegetables and bean sprouts. Cook, stirring, over a high heat for 3–4 minutes or until beginning to soften. Add the lemon juice and continue to cook briskly, stirring, until the vegetables are tender and most of the moisture has evaporated. Season and leave to cool.

3 Melt 50 g (2 oz) butter. Quarter the pastry sheets into 20 rectangles. Layer the pieces into six stacks of three, using up the two spare rectangles on any thin or split pastry stacks. Brush with the melted butter between each layer.

4 Divide the cool vegetable mixture between the six pastries. Draw the pastry edges up around the filling, pinching the tops together to form little 'money bags'. Place on a greased baking sheet and brush with more butter.

5 Bake in the oven at 200°C (400°F) mark 6 for about 20 minutes or until well browned and crisp. If necessary, cover the tops lightly with greaseproof paper to prevent overbrowning. Serve warm, garnished with parsley.

*130 Calories per serving*

# CHICKEN IN CIDER AND HONEY

*The part-boning of the chicken legs produces a neat shape; your local butcher will be happy to do this for you. It is optional, however, as the finished dish is just as good with whole chicken legs.*

6 chicken legs
3 Granny Smith apples
juice of 1 lemon
butter or margarine
225 g (8 oz) carrots, finely diced
125 g (4 oz) onion, skinned and finely diced
1 celery stick, finely diced
450 ml (¾ pint) medium-sweet cider
15 ml (1 tbsp) runny honey
1 bay leaf
salt and pepper
10 ml (2 level tsp) caster sugar
about 30 ml (2 tbsp) single cream

1  With the point of a small, sharp knife, work the chicken flesh free from the thigh end of each leg down to the central knee joint. Sever the thigh bones at the knee joint and remove. Cut the knuckles off the drumsticks. Wrap the boned flesh down around the drumsticks and tie securely at intervals with string.

2  Peel, halve and core the apples, reserving the peel. Cut each half into three wedges. Place the apple in a bowl with the lemon juice and toss together. Add enough cold water to cover, and refrigerate until required.

3  Melt 40 g (1½ oz) butter in a shallow flame-proof casserole. Fry the chicken legs over a moderate heat until they are a pale golden colour. Remove with a slotted spoon.

4  Stir the reserved apple peelings and the vegetables into the pan. Cook, stirring, over a medium heat for 10–15 minutes or until quite soft. Skim off all excess fat, then return the chicken to the pan. Add the cider, honey, bay leaf and seasoning and bring to the boil. Cover and cook in the oven at 200°C (400°F) mark 6 for about 30 minutes or until the chicken is cooked. (Test with a skewer; the juices should run clear.) The vegetables should be *very* tender.

5  Meanwhile, melt 25 g (1 oz) butter in a sauté pan. Drain the apple wedges and fry them with the sugar until golden. Cover and keep warm.

6  Spoon the chicken out of the pan, remove the string and keep warm. Remove the bay leaf, then purée the contents of the casserole in a food processor. Sieve into the rinsed-out casserole and boil to reduce slightly, if necessary. Remove from the heat.

7  Stir in the cream, adjust the seasoning, warm slightly, then pour or spoon over the chicken. Serve garnished with the apple wedges.

*300 Calories per serving*

---

# BRAISED BABY ONIONS

*The onions will stay whole if the root end is kept intact when skinning.*

30 ml (2 tbsp) olive oil
about 24 small onions, skinned
50 ml (2 fl oz) white wine
30 ml (2 level tbsp) chopped fresh parsley

1  Heat the oil in a flameproof casserole and sauté the onions for 3–4 minutes or until deep golden.

2  Add the wine and parsley and simmer gently, covered, for 15–20 minutes or until tender.

*40 Calories per serving*

---

# TOASTED POLENTA

*Polenta, or ground corn, is a staple of northern Italian cooking. It's often eaten hot, like porridge, but it can also be cooled, cut into squares and then fried or grilled, as here. Different types require varying cooking times; always ensure the mixture is tender and the liquid well reduced. The polenta squares can be prepared the day before.*

200 g (7 oz) polenta
5 ml (1 level tsp) salt
25 g (1 oz) butter
1 garlic clove, skinned and crushed
black pepper

1 In a saucepan, mix the polenta with 1.1 litres (2 pints) cold water. Add the salt and simmer for about 15 minutes or until very thick and no longer grainy. Stir frequently to prevent sticking.
2 Remove from the heat and stir in the butter, garlic and black pepper.
3 Turn the polenta out on to a wooden board or plate and spread to a thickness of about 1–2 cm (½–¾ inch). Cool, cover and chill in the fridge for at least 1 hour. Cut into 5 cm (2 inch) squares.
4 Toast the squares on both sides under a hot grill for 7–10 minutes. Serve at once or cover loosely and keep warm.

*150 Calories per serving*

# PEAS WITH LEEKS AND PANCETTA

*Pancetta is Italian seasoned bacon, available from good delicatessens.*

45 ml (3 tbsp) olive oil
125 g (4 oz) leeks, thinly sliced
25 g (1 oz) pancetta or streaky bacon
(about 2–3 thin slices), finely chopped
450 g (1 lb) petits pois
100 ml (4 fl oz) chicken or vegetable stock
salt and pepper

1 Heat the oil and cook the leeks and pancetta over a medium heat for 1–2 minutes.
2 Add the peas, stock and seasoning. (Remember the pancetta is salty.) Cover and simmer gently for 3–4 minutes or until the peas are cooked.

*100 Calories per serving*

# MUSCOVADO CREAMS

*This simple dessert originated at Prue Leith's School of Food and Wine. Try using it to top halved grapes.*

284 ml (10 fl oz) carton double cream
454 g (16 oz) carton Greek-style natural yogurt
142 g (5 oz) carton natural yogurt
about 90 ml (6 level tbsp) light Muscovado sugar

1 Whip the cream and fold in all the yogurt.
2 Spoon half the mixture into individual glasses and sprinkle with half the sugar. Add the remaining cream mixture, top with a layer of sugar and chill in the fridge overnight.

*385 Calories per serving*

# Coconut Crème Caramel

caster sugar
butter
568 ml (1 pint) milk
75 g (3 oz) block creamed coconut
3 whole eggs, plus 3 egg yolks
142 ml (5 fl oz) carton single cream
Tuiles (see right) and single cream, to serve

1 Put 175 g (6 oz) caster sugar in a medium heavy-based saucepan. Heat gently until the sugar has dissolved. Increase the heat and continue to cook until the mixture turns a golden caramel. Immediately pour the hot caramel into a shallow 1.1 litre (2 pint) ovenproof dish. Leave for 5 minutes to cool and set. Lightly butter the sides of the dish above the caramel to prevent it from going cloudy.

2 Place the milk in a medium saucepan and grate in the creamed coconut. Warm through gently until the coconut has dissolved completely.

3 Whisk the eggs and egg yolks together until evenly blended. Continue to whisk while adding the coconut milk, cream and 30 ml (2 level tbsp) caster sugar.

4 Strain the mixture into the dish on top of the caramel. Place in a roasting tin and pour in enough cold water to come halfway up the side of the dish. Bake, uncovered, in the oven at 170°C (325°F) mark 3 for about 1½ hours or until just set. Cool, cover, then chill over one or two nights until firm.

5 To serve, run the blade of a knife around the edge of the custard and turn out on to a serving plate. Serve with the Tuiles and single cream.

*450 Calories per serving*

# Tuiles

*These crisp biscuits are the perfect complement to the Muscovado Creams or Coconut Crème Caramel. They are also wonderful served with other mousses, ice creams or sorbets.*

25 g (1 oz) desiccated coconut
2 egg whites
65 g (2½ oz) icing sugar
65 g (2½ oz) plain flour
65 g (2½ oz) butter, melted

1 In a bowl, beat together the coconut, egg whites, icing sugar and flour. Mix in the melted butter.

2 Spoon four small spoonfuls of mixture on to a baking sheet lined with non-stick baking parchment. Smooth the mixture into thin 5 cm (2 inch) diameter rounds.

3 Bake in the oven at 230°C (450°F) mark 8 for 3–4 minutes. Remove the tuiles from the baking sheet with a palette knife while they are still warm. Immediately place each biscuit over a rolling pin to produce a curved shape, and leave to cool. Once set, ease the biscuits off the rolling pin. Repeat to make 12 biscuits. Store in an airtight tin until required.

MAKES ABOUT 12

*90 Calories per serving*

*Coconut Crème Caramel, Tuiles (above)*

# INFORMAL VEGETARIAN DINNER

---

## Menu

*Grilled Chicory with Pears and Hazelnuts*

---

*Roasted Pepper and Sweet Onion Pizzas*
*Rocket, Tomato and Sugar Snap Pea Salad*

---

*Cappuccino Creams* or *Tiramisù*

SERVES 8

---

This Italian-influenced dinner is easy to prepare in advance, or everything except the Tiramisù could be prepared from scratch in a couple of hours on the day. If you prefer not to serve a starter, the pizza recipe should be multiplied by one and a half. Individual pizzas look good, but might be difficult to fit into your oven, so we suggest that you make two large pizzas and divide each one into four. The rocket salad is deliciously fresh, cutting through the richness of the pizza. Follow with Cappuccino Creams or Tiramisù to complete the Italian mood of the meal.

---

## COUNTDOWN

**The day before**

Make the Cappuccino Creams or the Tiramisù, cover and refrigerate. Prepare the pizza toppings. Roast, skin and slice the peppers, cover and chill. Prepare the onions, soften, cool, cover and chill. Skin and slice the garlic, cover and chill. Skin and chop the tomatoes, cover and chill. Slice the mozzarella, cover and chill. Cook the sugar snap peas, cool, cover and chill. Make the dressing in a screw-topped jar. Wash and trim the rocket or watercress and store in a polythene bag in the fridge.

**On the day**

Make up the pizza dough, put it in a bowl and cover with a polythene bag. Refrigerate until 1 hour before required.

**To serve at 8 pm**

**6.45 pm:** Roll out the dough, slide on to baking sheets and scatter over the toppings. Leave in a warm place to prove. Grill the chicory, top with pears, cover and set aside. Place the rocket, tomatoes and sugar-snaps in a salad bowl.

**7.30 pm:** Take the Cappuccino Creams out of the fridge. Unwrap and decorate with chocolate curls.

**7.45 pm:** Put the chicory in the oven to reheat for 10 minutes. Drizzle the pizzas with oil. Tear the herbs for the pizza garnish. Dress and toss the salad.

**7.55 pm:** Put the pizzas in the oven while you eat your first course. If you forget to scatter the herbs while cooking, do it just as the pizzas come out of the oven.

---

> ### FREEZER NOTES
> *The pizza bases can be frozen. Roll out and open-freeze the bases until solid. Overwrap and freeze. Thaw for 1–2 hours at cool room temperature.*

---

# GRILLED CHICORY WITH PEARS AND HAZELNUTS

*Grilling the chicory transforms it by caramelising the juices. Pears brushed with hazelnut oil are the perfect foil to any bitterness the chicory may have.*

4 large or 8 small heads chicory, halved lengthways and cored
olive oil for basting
2 ripe pears, peeled, halved, cored and sliced
45 ml (3 tbsp) hazelnut oil
15 ml (1 level tbsp) chopped fresh thyme or 5 ml (1 level tsp) dried thyme
black pepper
50 g (2 oz) hazelnuts, toasted and chopped
sprigs of fresh thyme, to garnish

1 Brush the chicory all over with olive oil. Place in a grill pan, cut-side up, and cook under a very hot grill (as near to the heat as possible) for 3–4 minutes (2–3 minutes for smaller heads) or until just beginning to char and soften. Turn, baste with more oil and cook for a further 2–3 minutes (1–2 minutes for smaller heads).

2 Carefully turn the chicory again and top with slices of pear. Brush with hazelnut oil, sprinkle on the thyme, season with pepper and grill for 5–6 minutes (4–5 minutes for smaller heads). Carefully transfer the chicory (it will be very soft) to warmed plates. Scatter with the hazelnuts, garnish with extra sprigs of thyme and drizzle with the remaining hazelnut oil. Serve with crusty Italian bread.

*155 Calories per serving*

---

*Overleaf: Roasted Pepper and Sweet Onion Pizzas, Rocket, Tomato and Sugar Snap Pea Salad (page 48)*

# ROASTED PEPPER AND SWEET ONION PIZZAS

*These pretty pizzas are easy to make and the topping ingredients can be prepared in advance. Don't use ordinary onions – they will linger on the breath!*

4 large yellow or red peppers
olive oil
4 large white or red onions, skinned and sliced
three 283 g (10 oz) packets white bread and pizza mix
two 200 g (7 oz) mozzarella cheeses, sliced
two 397 g (14 oz) cans chopped tomatoes, well drained
6 garlic cloves, skinned and thinly sliced
salt and pepper
60 ml (4 tbsp) fresh oregano or basil leaves or 15 ml (1 tbsp) dried

1 Preheat the oven to 200°C (400°F) mark 6, or the grill to the hottest temperature. Bake or grill the peppers until blackening all over. Cover with a damp cloth and leave until cool enough to handle, then carefully peel off the skins. Remove and discard the stalks and seeds. Cut the flesh into thick strips.
2 Heat 60 ml (4 tbsp) olive oil in a frying pan and fry the onions gently for 5 minutes or until softened but not coloured. Set aside.
3 Make up the pizza dough following manufacturer's instructions, substituting 60 ml (4 tbsp) olive oil for the same amount of the liquid measurement. Divide in two and roll out into thin 30.5 cm (12 inch) rounds on a floured surface. Place each on a baking sheet.
4 Cover the pizza bases with the mozzarella. Spoon over the tomatoes, then scatter with the onions, peppers and garlic. Season with salt and pepper and drizzle with olive oil. Brush the edges of the pizza with oil. Leave in a warm place for 20–30 minutes or until the pizza bases have doubled in size.

5 Bake the pizzas in the oven for 15–20 minutes or until golden and bubbling. Scatter with the herbs 5 minutes before the pizzas are cooked. Serve immediately while still hot.

*505 Calories per serving*

# ROCKET, TOMATO AND SUGAR SNAP PEA SALAD

*A crisp and colourful salad to freshen the palate! If you can't find rocket (a peppery salad leaf much loved in Italy), use watercress for a similar flavour.*

350 g (12 oz) sugar snap peas, topped and tailed
225 g (8 oz) rocket (roquette)
450 g (1 lb) cherry tomatoes

FOR THE DRESSING
60 ml (4 tbsp) olive and sunflower oil, mixed
15 ml (1 tbsp) cider vinegar or lemon juice
5 ml (1 level tsp) whole grain mustard
salt and pepper
a pinch of sugar

1 Bring a pan of salted water to the boil and add the peas. Boil for 4 minutes, then drain and refresh in cold water to stop the cooking process and keep the colour. Pat dry on absorbent kitchen paper.
2 Mix all the vegetables together, halving the cherry tomatoes, if liked.
3 Whisk all the dressing ingredients together and pour over the vegetables, mixing well to coat. Serve immediately.

*105 Calories per serving*

# CAPPUCCINO CREAMS

*These little desserts are light but creamy and can be made with low-fat fromage frais if preferred. Use a good dark chocolate – the flavour is so much better.*

550 g (1¼ lb) fromage frais
15–30 ml (1–2 level tbsp) finely ground espresso coffee (see Cook's tip)
15–30 ml (1–2 level tbsp) icing sugar (optional)
175 g (6 oz) plain or bitter chocolate, broken into pieces
chocolate curls, to decorate

1 Mix the fromage frais with the coffee and icing sugar, if using.
2 Grind the chocolate in an electric blender or food processor until very fine. Alternatively, grate it finely.
3 Spoon half the fromage frais into eight individual ramekins or glass dishes. Sprinkle over most of the chocolate. Top with the remaining fromage frais and sprinkle with the remaining chocolate, giving a speckled appearance like a cappuccino. Decorate with chocolate curls.

*210 Calories per serving*

---

### COOK'S TIP

*The coffee used for Cappuccino Creams should be so finely ground that it is just a little more coarse than icing sugar – this is sold as Italian espresso coffee and is very strong. Alternatively, you can use pulverised Turkish coffee, which is not as strong and has a consistency similar to that of icing sugar.*

# TIRAMISÙ

*'Tiramisù' is an Italian word, meaning 'pick me up', describing the heady nature of this wickedly rich Venetian dessert. Tiramisù is incredibly quick and easy to make, but be sure to make it the day before required as it needs time for the layers to merge into one another and for the flavours to mature.*

four 250 g (9 oz) cartons mascarpone cheese
40 g (1½ oz) caster sugar
3 eggs, separated
250 ml (8 fl oz) Kahlua or other coffee-flavoured liqueur
425 ml (14 fl oz) very strong cold black coffee
about 30 savoiardi (Italian sponge fingers)
cocoa powder for dredging

1 Put the mascarpone cheese, sugar and egg yolks in a bowl and beat with an electric mixer until evenly blended and creamy.
2 Whisk the egg whites until standing in stiff peaks. Fold into the mascarpone mixture and spoon about one quarter into a glass serving bowl.
3 Mix the liqueur and coffee together in a shallow dish. Taking one at a time, dip 10 of the savoiardi in this mixture for 10–15 seconds, turning once so they become soaked through but do not lose their shape. Place each one on top of the mascarpone, making a single layer of savoiardi that covers the mascarpone completely.
4 Cover the savoiardi with one third of the remaining mascarpone, then dip another 10 savoiardi in the liqueur and coffee mixture. Layer them in the bowl as before.
5 Repeat with another layer of mascarpone and savoiardi, then spread the remaining mascarpone over the top and swirl with a palette knife. Sift cocoa powder liberally all over the top. Cover the bowl and refrigerate for 24 hours. Serve chilled.

*760 Calories per serving*

# VEGETARIAN
# FEAST

## Menu

*Spinach Parcels on a Tomato Coulis*

*Wild Mushroom Strudel with Brandy and Celery Sauce*
*Lamb's Lettuce and Asparagus Salad*
*New Potatoes*
*Julienne of Carrots and Parsnips*

*Fruits with Kirsch and Orange Cream*

SERVES 6

We invited a well-known vegetarian chef to give us her ideas for a dinner party menu. She came up with a menu that is not only light and full of flavour but looks good, too, 'showing how simple, delicious and imaginative this type of cuisine can be'.

## ——————— COUNTDOWN ———————

**The day before**
Make the Tomato Coulis, cool, cover and refrigerate. Prepare the Spinach Parcels to the end of step 4, then cover and refrigerate. Complete the strudel to the end of step 3, then cover and refrigerate. Make the Brandy and Celery Sauce to the end of step 3. Cool, cover

and refrigerate. Wash and dry the salad leaves. Cook the asparagus tips and cool. Pack separately into polythene bags. Prepare the dressing and store in a screw-topped jar. Peel and slice into fine strips 450 g (1 lb) each of carrots and parsnips, and refrigerate in polythene bags. Scrub 700 g (1½ lb) new potatoes. Cover with cold water and store in a cool place. Prepare the Orange Cream, cover and refrigerate. Prepare the fruit and mix with the Kirsch. Prepare the caramel shapes and store in an airtight container.

**To serve at 8 pm**
**6 pm:** Put the fruit together with the Orange Cream, cover and refrigerate.

**7.15 pm:** Preheat the oven to 220°C (425°F) mark 7. Assemble, but do not dress the salad; cover and refrigerate.

**7.30 pm:** Bake the strudel. Cook the potatoes, drain and keep warm.

**7.45 pm:** Simmer the carrots and parsnips until tender. Steam the Spinach Parcels and reheat the Coulis. Dress the salad and reheat the Brandy and Celery Sauce, adding the cream. Keep warm and add the brandy just before serving. Cover the strudel and keep warm.

**8 pm:** Decorate the dessert with caramel shapes. Serve the starter.

---

> ### FREEZER NOTES
> *Only the Tomato Coulis will freeze. Cool, pack and freeze. To use, thaw overnight at cool room temperature.*

---

## SPINACH PARCELS ON A TOMATO COULIS

*These parcels are equally delicious served warm or cold. If spinach is not available, you could use a round lettuce instead.*

350 g (12 oz) celeriac
salt and pepper
75 g (3 oz) Cheddar cheese, grated
25 g (1 oz) creamy fresh goat's cheese or full-fat soft cheese
15 ml (1 tbsp) olive oil
450 g (1 lb) ripe tomatoes, chopped
15 ml (1 level tbsp) tomato purée
a pinch of cayenne pepper
1 bay leaf
15 ml (1 level tbsp) chopped fresh basil
5 ml (1 level tsp) sugar

15–30 ml (1–2 tbsp) red wine
150 ml (¼ pint) vegetable stock
16 medium fresh spinach leaves (see Cook's tip)
fresh chives, to garnish (optional)

1  For the filling, peel and finely dice the celeriac and cook in boiling salted water for 12–15 minutes or until tender. Drain, mash and beat in the Cheddar, goat's cheese and seasoning. Leave to cool.

2  Meanwhile, make the Tomato Coulis. Heat the olive oil in a medium saucepan, add the tomatoes, cover and cook until soft. Uncover, bring to the boil and add the tomato purée, cayenne pepper, bay leaf, basil, sugar, red wine and stock. Simmer for 10–15 minutes. Remove the bay leaf and blend in a food processor until smooth. Sieve, then season to taste. Pour into a pan.

3  Wash the spinach leaves and steam for 4–6 minutes or until tender. Drain on a wire rack.

4  To finish, lay two spinach leaves, slightly overlapping, on a work surface. Place one sixth of the filling on top and wrap to enclose it. Repeat to make six parcels. If wished, tie a fresh chive around each parcel.

5  Steam the parcels gently for about 10 minutes or until heated through. Reheat the Coulis and pour a little on to each plate. Place a Spinach Parcel on top.

*110 Calories per serving*

---

> ### COOK'S TIP
> *As there is quite a lot of filling in each parcel, steam a few extra spinach leaves in case some tear or split.*

---

# WILD MUSHROOM STRUDEL

*This savoury strudel relies on the use of wild mush-rooms. Shiitake mushrooms are available fresh from some supermarkets. Alternatively, order them from your greengrocer or replace them with fresh oyster mushrooms. If fresh wild mushrooms are not avail-able, soak 25 g (1 oz) dried porcini mushrooms for 2 hours in cold water, strain and substitute for 125 g (4 oz) of the total weight.*

225 g (8 oz) long-grain brown rice
salt and pepper
450 g (1 lb) mixed mushrooms, such as shiitake, morel, flat and field
butter
450 g (1 lb) leeks, finely chopped
65 g (2½ oz) walnut pieces, finely chopped
10 ml (2 level tsp) chopped fresh oregano
20 ml (4 tsp) tamari or soy sauce
5 ml (1 level tsp) yeast extract
4 sheets filo pastry, each measuring about 45.5×28 cm (18×11 inches)
sesame seeds
Brandy and Celery Sauce, to serve

1  Cook the rice in boiling salted water until tender. Drain and cool. Finely sliver the shi-itake and morel mushrooms and roughly chop the flat and field mushrooms.

2  Melt 25 g (1 oz) butter in a large frying pan. Add the leeks and fry for 1–2 minutes. Stir in the mushrooms and continue cooking for about 8 minutes or until quite tender and all excess moisture is driven off. Mix in the wal-nuts, oregano, tamari, yeast extract, rice and seasoning. Turn out into a bowl and cool.

3  Melt 40 g (1½ oz) butter. Layer up three sheets of pastry, brushing butter on top of each sheet. Cut in half crossways. Spoon the filling over the two stacks of sheets, leaving a narrow strip around the sides of each. Fold in the sides

and roll up the strudels. Transfer to a lightly greased baking sheet. Brush the outside with melted butter and crumple the remaining pas-try on top. Brush with the remaining butter and sprinkle with sesame seeds.

4  Bake in the oven at 220°C (425°F) mark 7 for 25–30 minutes or until the pastry is crisp and golden. Serve accompanied by the Brandy and Celery Sauce.

*300 Calories per serving*

---

# BRANDY AND CELERY SAUCE

*This sauce has a very attractive speckled appearance. If you're nervous of igniting the brandy, simply add it to the sauce and boil for a further 1–2 minutes.*

25 g (1 oz) butter or margarine
4 celery sticks, finely diced
15 ml (1 level tbsp) rice flour or plain flour
300 ml (½ pint) vegetable stock
15 ml (1 level tbsp) chopped fresh dill or 5 ml (1 level tsp) dried dill weed
salt and pepper
142 ml (5 fl oz) carton single cream
15–30 ml (1–2 tbsp) brandy
chopped fresh dill, to garnish

1  Heat the butter in a saucepan, add the celery and cook gently until almost tender.

2  Stir in the flour and cook for 1 minute. Remove from the heat, gradually blend in the stock, and bring to the boil, stirring all the time. Mix in the dill and seasoning and simmer for about 5 minutes. Cool slightly.

3  Purée the sauce in a food processor, then sieve into a clean saucepan.

4  Whisk the cream into the sauce and heat

until boiling, stirring occasionally. Adjust the seasoning.

5 Gently heat the brandy until warm, but not boiling. Remove from the heat, set alight and stir into the sauce. Garnish with fresh dill.

*100 Calories per serving*

———— ❧ ————

# L AMB'S LETTUCE AND ASPARAGUS SALAD

*Make sure you add the dressing to the salad only just before serving.*

1 red pepper
a few fresh asparagus tips
salt and pepper
about 18 leaves lamb's lettuce
½ small frisée lettuce
1 small oakleaf lettuce
30 ml (2 tbsp) walnut oil
30 ml (2 tbsp) white wine vinegar
5 ml (1 level tsp) whole grain mustard
15 ml (1 level tbsp) chopped fresh dill

1 Grill the pepper until well charred all over; the skin should have blistered and be plumped up. Cover with a cloth and leave to cool for 10–15 minutes. Peel, de-seed and cut the pepper into strips. Cook the asparagus tips in boiling, salted water until tender. Drain and cool.

2 Rinse and drain the salad leaves and roughly chop the frisée and oakleaf lettuce. Mix with the red pepper.

3 Whisk together the oil, vinegar, mustard, dill and seasoning, and toss with the salad ingredients just before serving. Garnish the salad with the asparagus tips.

*45 Calories per serving*

# F RUITS WITH KIRSCH AND ORANGE CREAM

*Use clear glasses to show this dessert to its best advantage. It is very quick and easy to make.*

2 large oranges
284 ml (10 fl oz) carton double cream
3 large, ripe peaches
1 small pineapple
15 ml (1 tbsp) Kirsch
caramel shapes (see Cook's tip), to decorate

1 Grate the rind from the oranges. Whip the cream until it just holds its shape and fold in the rind. Peel and segment the oranges. Wipe, quarter, stone and slice the peaches. Chop the pineapple flesh. Mix all the fruits together and stir in the Kirsch.

2 Divide the fruits between six individual glasses. Top with the orange cream and decorate with caramel shapes.

*290 Calories per serving*

---

### COOK'S TIP

*To make caramel shapes, place 75 g (3 oz) granulated sugar in a small saucepan. Heat gently until the sugar has dissolved, then increase the heat until it turns a golden caramel. Drizzle caramel from the end of a fork into irregular shapes on lightly oiled foil. Leave the shapes to set at room temperature before peeling off the foil.*

---

———— ❧ ————

*Overleaf (left to right): Lamb's Lettuce and Asparagus Salad (above), Wild Mushroom Strudel (page 52), Brandy and Celery Sauce (page 52), new potatoes, julienne of carrots and parsnips*

# *I*TALIAN SUPPER WITH FRIENDS

## Menu

*Aubergine and Red Pepper Roulade*

*Hot Carpaccio with Salsa Verde*
*Pasta with Courgette and Carrot Ribbons*
*French Beans with Feta and Tomatoes*

*Zuccotto*

SERVES 6

This unusual menu is ideal to share with close friends, as the food needs some attention between courses. The Aubergine and Red Pepper Roulade can be prepared well ahead, but the Carpaccio has to be cooked at the last minute.

While it's in the oven, your guests can help themselves to the elegant pasta dish and the delicious combination of French Beans with Feta and Tomatoes. Finish with Zuccotto – a deliciously rich and alcoholic Florentine version of Tipsy Cake.

## ——— COUNTDOWN ———

**The day before**
Prepare the roulade to the end of step 6. Make the sesame relish and prepare the beef to the end of step 2. Cover all and refrigerate. Make the carrot and courgette ribbons. Keep, covered, in a bowl of cold water in the fridge. Top and tail the French beans. Store in a polythene bag in the fridge. Chop the thyme for the pasta and store as for the beans. Make the Zuccotto.

**On the day**
Make the Salsa Verde, cover and keep in a cool place. Crumble the feta cheese, cover and refrigerate. Slice the sun-dried tomatoes thinly, cover and keep in a cool place.

**To serve at 8 pm**

**7.20 pm:** Slice the roulade and arrange on plates with a spoonful of relish. Cover and leave at room temperature. Place the meat on two large baking sheets. Cover.

**7.40 pm:** Preheat the oven to 240°C (475°F) mark 9. Cook the pasta and beans as directed. Keep warm in covered serving dishes.

**8 pm:** Serve the starter. Between courses, cook the Carpaccio.

---

> ### FREEZER NOTES
> *The recipes in this menu are not suitable for freezing.*

---

# Aubergine and red pepper roulade

2 medium red peppers, about 300 g (11 oz) total weight

1 medium, long aubergine, about 300 g (11 oz) total weight

olive oil

10 ml (2 level tsp) coriander seeds, crushed

salt and pepper

fresh basil leaves, to garnish

### FOR THE SESAME RELISH

25 g (1 oz) sesame seeds

25 g (1 oz) fresh basil, stalks removed

25 g (1 oz) Parmesan cheese, freshly grated

1 garlic clove, skinned

15 ml (1 tbsp) sesame oil

olive oil

1 Cut a piece of greaseproof paper into a rectangle measuring about 35.5×30.5 cm (14×12 inches).

2 Grill the peppers under a hot grill, turning occasionally, for about 20 minutes or until the skin is charred.

3 Slice the aubergine lengthways as thinly as possible. Brush liberally with olive oil and place on the grill pan. Grill in batches for about 2–3 minutes on both sides or until softened and slightly charred. Drain on absorbent kitchen paper.

4 Place the aubergine slices lengthways in a single layer on the greaseproof paper, overlapping the slices by about 1 cm (½ inch) to form a rectangle measuring about 35.5×18 cm (14×7 inches). Sprinkle over half the crushed coriander seeds, then season.

5 Remove the stalks, seeds and skins from the peppers under cold water. Cut the peppers into quarters and lay over the aubergines, overlapping as before. Sprinkle with the remaining coriander. Season.

6 Use the greaseproof paper to help you to roll the roulade up tightly, from a short side, like a Swiss roll. Wrap and chill overnight in the fridge.

7 To make the sesame relish, place the sesame seeds in a dry saucepan and stir over a medium heat until starting to turn golden brown. Tip into a food processor with the remaining relish ingredients and 50 ml (2 fl oz) olive oil. Process until smooth. Spoon into a jar, cover with a layer of olive oil and store in the fridge. Bring both relish and roulade to room temperature before serving.

8 To serve, unwrap the roulade and slice thinly with a very sharp knife. Place two or three slices on each of six small plates. Spoon a generous serving of relish on the side and garnish the roulade with fresh basil leaves.

*250 Calories per serving*

# *H*OT CARPACCIO WITH SALSA VERDE

*Try our version of an Italian favourite. It's cooked in a flash, so be careful not to overcook the succulently tender beef.*

450 g (1 lb) fillet of beef
90 ml (6 tbsp) olive oil
30 ml (2 tbsp) dark soy sauce
black pepper

FOR THE SALSA VERDE
3 anchovy fillets in oil, drained
2 garlic cloves, skinned and crushed
2.5 ml (½ tsp) balsamic or sherry vinegar
15 ml (1 level tbsp) roughly chopped capers
60 ml (4 level tbsp) chopped fresh parsley
150 ml (¼ pint) olive oil
black pepper

1 With a sharp knife, cut the beef into twelve 0.5 cm (¼ inch) slices. Bat out each slice between damp greaseproof paper until it has doubled in size and is almost transparent. Be careful not to tear the meat. Lay the slices of beef in a non-metallic dish.

2 Whisk together the olive oil, soy sauce and plenty of black pepper. Pour this over the meat. Cover and leave to marinate for at least 2 hours, preferably overnight, in the fridge, turning once.

3 Meanwhile, to make the salsa verde, pound the anchovies in a pestle and mortar or in a strong bowl with the end of a rolling pin. Stir in the garlic and the vinegar. Beat in the chopped capers and parsley, then gradually add the olive oil. Season with pepper. (You should not need to add any salt as the anchovies are salty.)

4 Preheat the oven to 240°C (475°F) mark 9. (The oven must be very hot for this recipe.) Lay the meat in a single layer on two large baking sheets and bake for 2 minutes only, until it has

changed colour to brown. Transfer the meat to warm plates and serve immediately, dressed with a little salsa verde.

*500 Calories per serving*

---

### COOK'S TIP

*To make it easier to cut the beef into slices, place it in the freezer beforehand and leave for up to 30 minutes to firm up. Alternatively, simply ask the butcher to slice it for you. The Carpaccio can also be served cut into strips, with the salsa as a dip – great for parties.*

---

# *P*ASTA WITH COURGETTE AND CARROT RIBBONS

175 g (6 oz) courgettes
175 g (6 oz) carrots, peeled
225 g (8 oz) broad ribbon pasta
salt and pepper
40 g (1½ oz) butter
2.5 ml (½ level tsp) chopped fresh thyme

1 Using a swivel peeler, carefully pare the courgettes and carrots into ribbons.

2 Cook the pasta in boiling salted water, adding the vegetable ribbons 1 minute before the end of the cooking time. Drain and toss with the butter and thyme. Season.

*195 Calories per serving*

---

*Left to right: Hot Carpaccio with Salsa Verde (above), Pasta with Courgette and Carrot Ribbons (above), French Beans with Feta and Tomatoes (page 60)*

# FRENCH BEANS WITH FETA AND TOMATOES

*If you cannot find sun-dried tomatoes, use 125 g (4 oz) de-seeded fresh tomatoes, cut into strips. If using loose sun-dried tomatoes (not packed in oil), soak in boiling water for 15 minutes first.*

350 g (12 oz) fine French beans, topped, tailed and halved
salt and pepper
50 g (2 oz) sun-dried tomatoes
125 g (4 oz) feta or Wensleydale cheese
15 ml (1 tbsp) olive oil

1 Cook the beans in boiling salted water for about 6 minutes, then drain.
2 Meanwhile, cut the sun-dried tomatoes lengthways into slices. Crumble the cheese.
3 While the beans are still hot, toss them with the sun-dried tomatoes, cheese and olive oil. Season to taste, remembering that the feta is salty. Serve immediately.

*80 Calories per serving*

# ZUCCOTTO

50 g (2 oz) blanched almonds
50 g (2 oz) hazelnuts
45 ml (3 tbsp) brandy
30 ml (2 tbsp) orange-flavoured liqueur
30 ml (2 tbsp) cherry- or almond-flavoured liqueur
350 g (12 oz) trifle sponges or Madeira cake
150 g (5 oz) plain chocolate
450 ml (¾ pint) double cream
150 g (5 oz) icing sugar
25 g (1 oz) cocoa powder, to decorate

1 Spread the almonds and hazelnuts out separately on a baking tray and toast in the oven at 200°C (400°F) mark 6 for 5 minutes or until golden.
2 Transfer the hazelnuts to a clean tea-towel and rub off the skins while still warm. Spread all the nuts out to cool for 5 minutes, then chop roughly.
3 Line a 1.4 litre (2½ pint) pudding basin or round-bottomed bowl with damp muslin or a damp blue J-cloth. In a separate bowl, mix together the brandy and the liqueurs and set aside.
4 Split the trifle sponges in half through the middle. (If using Madeira cake, cut into 1 cm/ ½ inch slices.) Sprinkle with the brandy and liqueurs.
5 Line the basin with the moistened split sponges, reserving enough to cover the top.
6 Using a sharp knife, chop 75 g (3 oz) of the plain chocolate into small pieces and set aside.
7 In a separate bowl, whip the cream with 125 g (4 oz) icing sugar until stiff and fold in the chopped chocolate and nuts.
8 Divide this mixture in two and use one half to spread over the sponge lining in an even layer.
9 Melt the remaining chocolate in a heatproof bowl over a saucepan of simmering water, then leave to cool slightly. Fold the melted chocolate into the remaining cream mixture. Use this to fill the centre of the pudding.
10 Level the top of the zuccotto and cover with the remaining moistened sponge. Trim the edges. Cover and refrigerate for 12 hours.
11 To serve, uncover the zuccotto and invert a flat serving plate over the basin. Turn upside-down, lift off the bowl, and carefully remove the muslin. Serve cold, dusted with the remaining icing sugar and the cocoa powder.

*902 Calories per serving*

# *P*ERFECT SUMMER SUPPER

## *Menu*

### *Smoked Fish and Ricotta Toasts*

---

### *Honeyed Pork Riblets*
### *Saffron Mixed Grains*
### *Sweet Pepper Relish*
### *Baked Artichokes*

---

### *Tart of Many Fruits*

SERVES 6

Summer entertaining should be easy and relaxed. If the weather is good, cook the Honeyed Pork Riblets on the barbecue, with the Baked Artichokes. The Smoked Fish and Ricotta Toasts can be partly prepared the day before, and our classic dessert is sure to be a great success – a crisp, sweet pastry crust filled with smooth, rich crème pâtissière topped with a mound of glistening fresh summer fruits. You can choose whatever fruits are available to make a mouthwatering, colourful combination.

---
## COUNTDOWN
---

### The day before
Prepare the aubergine for the Smoked Fish and Ricotta Toasts. Cool, cover and refrigerate. Boil the quail's eggs, then shell. Cover and refrigerate. Prepare the Honeyed Pork Riblets to the end of step 2 and marinate in the fridge. Make the Sweet Pepper Relish. Cool, cover and refrigerate. Make the pastry case for the tart, cool and store in an airtight container. Make the crème pâtissière and refrigerate. Prepare the artichokes to the end of step 2. Cover and refrigerate.

### On the day
### To serve at 8 pm
**5.30 pm:** Fill the pastry case with the crème pâtissière and decorate with the fresh fruit. Make the glaze and brush the tart. Leave in the refrigerator until ready to serve.

61

**6 pm:** Sauté the onion for the Mixed Grains.

**7 pm:** Preheat the oven to 200°C (400°F) mark 6, or light the grill or barbecue. Make the toast for the starter.

**7.30 pm:** Assemble the Smoked Fish and Ricotta Toasts, but don't pour over the dressing yet.

**7.45 pm:** Put the Mixed Grains on to cook. Reheat the Sweet Pepper Relish, if serving hot. Place the artichokes in the oven or on the grill or barbecue. Cook the pork riblets on the grill or barbecue.

**8 pm:** Spoon the dressing over the Smoked Fish and Ricotta Toasts and serve.

### FREEZER NOTES

*All of the dishes in this menu, except the baked pastry case, are unsuitable for freezing. Bake the case as directed, cool and freeze for up to 3 months. Thaw at room temperature for 3–4 hours. If liked, re-crisp in a warm oven for a few minutes, cool and use as directed.*

*Tart of Many Fruits (page 66)*

# Smoked Fish and Ricotta Toasts

*We used smoked halibut but you could use cooked peeled prawns or more smoked salmon. Try using pesto sauce instead of mayonnaise.*

1 small aubergine, about 175 g (6 oz)
75 ml (3 fl oz) olive oil
1 small baguette
30 ml (2 level tbsp) mayonnaise
125 g (4 oz) ricotta cheese
salt and black pepper
25 ml (1 fl oz) white wine vinegar
30 ml (2 level tbsp) chopped fresh thyme
75 g (3 oz) smoked salmon
75 g (3 oz) smoked halibut
12 soft-boiled quail's eggs, shelled and halved, or
4 soft-boiled hen's eggs, shelled and quartered
sprigs of fresh thyme, to garnish

1 Cut the aubergine into wafer-thin slices. Brush both sides with a little of the olive oil and grill until golden brown and very crisp. Leave to cool.
2 Slice the baguette into 12 slices about 2.5 cm (1 inch) thick. Toast lightly on both sides. Spread one side with the mayonnaise.
3 Thinly slice the ricotta cheese and season with black pepper. Whisk together the remaining olive oil, vinegar, thyme and seasoning.
4 Arrange the smoked fish, aubergine, ricotta slices and quail's eggs on the toasts. Spoon over the dressing, garnish with thyme and serve immediately.

*300 Calories per serving*

# Honeyed Pork Riblets

900 g (2 lb) pork spare ribs
grated rind and juice of 2 oranges
15 ml (1 level tbsp) light brown sugar
15 ml (1 tbsp) white wine vinegar
15 ml (1 level tbsp) tomato purée
15 ml (1 tbsp) soy sauce
5 ml (1 tsp) Worcestershire sauce
60 ml (4 tbsp) tomato ketchup
45 ml (3 tbsp) runny honey
salt and pepper
15 ml (1 tbsp) Hoisin sauce (optional)

1 Place the spare ribs in a large saucepan, cover with cold water and bring slowly to the boil. Drain, discarding the liquid. Cover with fresh water and return to the boil. Cover and simmer for about 1 hour. Drain and cool.
2 Mix together the grated orange rind and strained juice with all the remaining ingredients. Stir into the riblets. Cover, refrigerate and leave to marinate for at least 1 hour, preferably overnight.
3 Cook the ribs on the barbecue or under a grill for 10–12 minutes, turning and basting with excess marinade, until they are well browned and heated through.

*90 Calories per serving*

# SAFFRON MIXED GRAINS

*'Gourmet Mixed Grains' is a delicious combination of long-grain brown, wehani, black japonica and wild rices. Look out for it in good supermarkets. If unavailable, use a mixture of long-grain brown and wild rice.*

30 ml (2 tbsp) olive oil
1 medium onion, skinned and finely chopped
225 g (8 oz) Gourmet Mixed Grains
5 ml (1 tsp) saffron strands
salt and pepper
75 g (3 oz) toasted pine nuts
75 g (3 oz) butter

1 Heat the oil in a large saucepan and sauté the onion until softened.
2 Add the mixed grains, saffron and 700 ml (24 fl oz) water with salt to taste. Bring to the boil, then reduce the heat, cover with a tightly fitting lid and simmer for about 35 minutes or until the grains are tender and the water is absorbed.
3 Stir in the pine nuts and butter and season generously with salt and pepper. Serve hot.

*355 Calories per serving*

# SWEET PEPPER RELISH

45 ml (3 tbsp) olive oil
3 large red or yellow peppers, about 450 g (1 lb) total weight, de-seeded and finely chopped
75 g (3 oz) shallots or onion, skinned and finely chopped
200 ml (7 fl oz) chicken or vegetable stock
salt and pepper
200 ml (7 fl oz) dry white wine
30 ml (2 level tbsp) caster sugar

1 Heat the olive oil in a medium saucepan and sauté the peppers and shallots until just beginning to soften.
2 Add all the remaining ingredients and bubble for 15–20 minutes or until the mixture is soft. Season and serve hot or cold.

*110 Calories per serving*

# BAKED ARTICHOKES

*If you're barbecuing the pork, the artichokes can be finished off on the grill, too. Cook for 20 minutes, as below, brushing occasionally with olive oil.*

6 small globe artichokes
salt and pepper
90 ml (6 tbsp) olive oil
lemon slices, to serve

1 Trim the artichoke stalks close to the base. Cook the artichokes whole, in boiling salted water, for about 30 minutes or until you can pull away a base leaf easily. Drain and refresh under cold water.
2 Halve the artichokes lengthways. With a small spoon, remove the 'hairy' choke.
3 Place the artichokes, cut-side uppermost, on a baking sheet. Drizzle with olive oil and season. Bake in the oven at 200°C (400°F) mark 6 for 15–20 minutes. Serve with slices of lemon.

*110 Calories per serving*

# TART OF MANY FRUITS

*This generously proportioned tart allows for second helpings. It can also be served without the glaze and decorated simply with a dusting of icing sugar.*

### FOR THE CRÈME PÂTISSIÈRE
568 ml (1 pint) milk
1 vanilla pod
4 eggs
75 g (3 oz) caster sugar
60 ml (4 level tbsp) plain flour
75 ml (5 level tbsp) cornflour
284 ml (10 fl oz) carton double cream

### FOR THE PASTRY
175 g (6 oz) plain flour
a pinch of salt
75 g (3 oz) caster sugar
125 g (4 oz) butter, chilled
1 egg, beaten

### FOR THE FILLING AND GLAZE
a selection of fresh fruits in season, prepared as necessary
135 ml (9 tbsp) apricot conserve
45 ml (3 tbsp) orange-flavoured liqueur
15 ml (1 tbsp) orangeflower water

1 Put the milk and vanilla pod in a heavy-based saucepan and heat gently until just boiling. Remove from the heat and leave to infuse for 30 minutes.

2 To make the pastry, sift the flour and salt together on to a clean surface. Make a well in the centre and add the sugar, butter and egg. Using the fingertips of one hand, pinch and work the sugar, butter and egg together until well blended.

3 Gradually work in all the flour, adding a little water if necessary to bind together. Knead lightly until the dough is smooth, then wrap in cling film and leave to rest in the refrigerator for about 1 hour.

4 When the milk has infused for at least 30 minutes, make the crème pâtissière. Cream the eggs and sugar together until very pale and thick.

5 Sift the flour and cornflour into a bowl, then gradually add a little of the milk to make a smooth paste. Gradually beat the flour mixture into the egg mixture.

6 Remove the vanilla pod from the milk, then reheat until just boiling. Pour on to the egg mixture, in a steady stream, stirring all the time.

7 Strain the mixture back into the saucepan. Reheat gently, stirring all the time, until the custard coats the back of a spoon. Pour the custard into a clean bowl, cover the top with a piece of damp greaseproof paper and leave to cool.

8 Roll out the pastry on a lightly floured surface and use to line a greased 28 cm (11 inch) fluted, round, loose-based flan tin. Cover and chill in the refrigerator for at least 30 minutes.

9 Bake the pastry case blind in the oven at 190°C (375°F) mark 5 for 15–20 minutes. Remove the baking beans and greaseproof paper and cook for a further 10 minutes or until the base is cooked through. Cool on a wire rack.

10 When both the pastry and the crème pâtissière are cool, remove the pastry case from the tin and place on a large flat serving plate or platter. Lightly whip the cream and fold into the crème pâtissière. Fill the pastry case with the mixture. Arrange the fruit on top, allowing some of it to tumble over the edge.

11 To make the glaze, gently heat the apricot conserve with the liqueur and orangeflower water. Do not boil. Brush the tart generously with the glaze. Serve on a large platter surrounded by fresh flowers, leaves and fruits.

*865 Calories per serving*

# $M$IDSUMMER DELIGHT

---

## Menu

*Summer Garden Soup*

---

*Glazed Lemon Chicken*
*Wild Rice and Thyme Salad*
*Mixed Leaf and Pine Nut Salad*
*Hot Savoury Bread*

---

*Currant Compote and Madeleines*

SERVES 8

---

Exciting and unusual flavours unite to create this delicious summer dinner party menu. It's a make-ahead menu with a lot to prepare in advance, but on the day you simply have to put it all together. To start, the Summer Garden Soup is served ice cold, chilled by the last-minute addition of crushed, minted ice cubes. Its gentle flavour is the ideal foil for the main course – chicken fillets steeped in lemon juice and finished with a golden sugar topping. It's served with an exotic salad of wild rice and thyme, tossed with summer beans and wild mushrooms. Our suggested dessert is light and refreshing – an irresistible Currant Compote served with delicious home-made Madeleines.

## ——— COUNTDOWN ———

**Two days before**
Make the chicken stock, cool, cover and refrigerate. Make the fresh mint ice cubes. Marinate the chicken. Make the salad dressings and store both in screw-topped jars in a cool place. Prepare the Hot Savoury Bread, wrap tightly in foil and store in the refrigerator.

**The day before**
Make the soup, cool, cover and refrigerate. Lightly crush the ice cubes and return to the freezer in a polythene bag. Cook and grill the chicken breast fillets, cover and refrigerate. Make the lemon mayonnaise sauce, cover and

67

refrigerate. Complete the Wild Rice and Thyme Salad, cover and refrigerate. Wash the salad leaves and alfalfa sprouts. Store in the fridge in a polythene bag. Toast the pine nuts and store in a cool place. Make the Currant Compote and refrigerate. Make the Madeleines and store in polythene bags.

**To serve at 8 pm**
**About 6.30 pm:** Remove the Currant Compote from the refrigerator.
**7 pm:** Assemble the Glazed Lemon Chicken with the Wild Rice and Thyme Salad. Coat with the lemon mayonnaise sauce. Prepare the soup garnishes.
**7.35 pm:** Heat the bread. Put the dressing for the Mixed Leaf and Pine Nut Salad in the bottom of the salad bowl. Place the salad leaves, alfalfa sprouts and pine nuts on top and return to the refrigerator. Do not mix until ready to serve.
**8 pm:** Serve the soup.

---

### FREEZER NOTES
*Freeze the soup; thaw overnight in the refrigerator. Stir well before using. Wrap and freeze the Hot Savoury Bread. Heat from frozen at 200°C (400°F) mark 6 for 45–50 minutes. Freeze the Madeleines in a rigid container. Thaw at cool room temperature for about 30 minutes. Freeze the Currant Compote in a rigid container. Thaw overnight in the refrigerator.*

# SUMMER GARDEN SOUP

*A good home-made chicken stock makes a world of difference to the flavour of this refreshing soup. Do remember to cool and chill the stock so that the fat can be skimmed off.*

50 g (2 oz) butter
50 g (2 oz) onion, skinned and finely chopped
1 bunch watercress, roughly chopped
½ round lettuce, roughly chopped
½ cucumber, about 175 g (6 oz), peeled and chopped
125 g (4 oz) potato, peeled and chopped
1 litre (1¾ pints) jellied chicken stock
142 ml (5 fl oz) carton single cream
salt and pepper
fresh mint ice cubes (see Cook's tip), watercress sprigs and cucumber slices, to garnish

1  Melt the butter in a large saucepan and sauté the onion for 2–3 minutes or until soft and golden. Stir in the watercress, lettuce, cucumber and potato. Sauté for a further 2 minutes before adding the chicken stock. Bring to the boil, cover and simmer for 15–20 minutes or until the potato is very soft. Cool.
2  Purée the mixture in a blender or food processor. Press through a sieve into a medium-sized bowl. Stir in the cream and seasoning. Cover and chill for at least 2 hours.
3  Garnish with crushed ice cubes, watercress sprigs and cucumber slices.

*105 Calories per serving*

### COOK'S TIP
*To make clear mint ice cubes, simply stir 30 ml (2 level tbsp) chopped fresh mint into 300 ml (½ pint) distilled water. Pour into ice-cube trays and freeze until solid. Place in a clean tea-towel and crush lightly with a rolling pin.*

# Glazed Lemon Chicken

8 skinless chicken breast fillets

about 6 large lemons

1 large garlic clove, skinned and crushed

1 cm (½ inch) piece of fresh root ginger, peeled and sliced

45–60 ml (3–4 tbsp) oil

75 ml (3 fl oz) chicken stock

about 50 g (2 oz) light soft brown sugar

75 ml (5 level tbsp) mayonnaise

142 ml (5 fl oz) carton soured cream

50 ml (2 fl oz) milk

salt and pepper

fresh thyme sprigs and lemon slices, to garnish

1 Place the chicken in a large, non-metallic bowl. Grate the rind of three lemons and reserve.

2 Squeeze the juice from the lemons to give 200 ml (7 fl oz). Pour over the chicken. Add the garlic and ginger. Mix well, cover with cling film and marinate in the fridge overnight.

3 Drain the chicken, reserving the marinade. Pat dry with absorbent kitchen paper.

4 Heat half the oil in a large, non-stick frying pan and brown the chicken, a few pieces at a time. Add more oil as necessary. Remove the chicken and wipe the pan free of any excess oil.

5 Return the chicken to the pan and pour over the marinade and stock. Simmer, covered, for 10–12 minutes. Cool in the liquid.

6 Transfer the chicken to a foil-lined grill pan, plump-side uppermost. Sprinkle with 10 ml (2 level tsp) reserved lemon rind and the sugar. Grill until golden and caramelised. Cool.

7 Beat together the mayonnaise, soured cream, remaining lemon rind, milk and seasoning. Cover and refrigerate. When cold, serve the chicken on a bed of Wild Rice and Thyme Salad. Coat lightly with lemon mayonnaise sauce and garnish with thyme and lemon.

*305 Calories per serving*

# Wild Rice and Thyme Salad

150 g (5 oz) French beans, topped, tailed and halved

salt and pepper

150 g (5 oz) shelled broad beans

50 g (2 oz) wild rice

175 g (6 oz) long-grain rice

50 ml (2 fl oz) grapeseed oil

50 g (2 oz) chanterelle, trompets des morts or small button mushrooms, roughly sliced

30 ml (2 level tbsp) chopped fresh thyme

25 ml (1 fl oz) walnut oil

30 ml (2 tbsp) white wine vinegar

15 ml (1 level tbsp) Dijon mustard

1 Cook the French beans in boiling salted water for 10–12 minutes or until they are just tender. Drain and refresh under cold water and set aside to cool completely.

2 Cook the broad beans in boiling salted water for 5–7 minutes. Drain and refresh under cold water, slipping off their outer skins if wished, and set aside to cool completely.

3 Place the wild rice in a large pan of boiling salted water. Boil for 25 minutes before adding the long-grain rice. Boil together for a further 10 minutes or until both are just tender. Drain and refresh the rice under cold water.

4 Stir together the French beans, broad beans and rice in a large mixing bowl.

5 Heat the grapeseed oil in a small sauté pan and sauté the mushrooms with the thyme for 2–3 minutes. Off the heat, stir in the walnut oil, vinegar, mustard and seasoning. Spoon into the rice mixture and stir well. Adjust the seasoning, cool, cover and refrigerate until required.

*250 Calories per serving*

# MIXED LEAF AND PINE NUT SALAD

*For the freshest salad, remember to toss the leaves and dressing together at the very last minute.*

1 small head radicchio
a small bunch lamb's tongue lettuce
½ head oakleaf lettuce
½ head frisée lettuce
25–50 g (1–2 oz) alfalfa sprouts
50 ml (2 fl oz) grapeseed oil
30 ml (2 tbsp) white wine vinegar
10 ml (2 tsp) runny honey
salt and pepper
25 g (1 oz) pine nuts, toasted

1 Wash the salad leaves and shred roughly. Rinse the alfalfa sprouts in a sieve or colander. Pat the salad leaves and the alfalfa sprouts dry with absorbent kitchen paper.
2 Whisk together the grapeseed oil, white wine vinegar and honey. Season.
3 In a large salad bowl, toss together the salad leaves, alfalfa sprouts, pine nuts and dressing. Serve immediately.

*85 Calories per serving*

# HOT SAVOURY BREAD

*Dark rye bread has a pungent flavour. For a lighter taste, try one of the paler-coloured ryes.*

1 large garlic clove, skinned and crushed
15 ml (1 level tbsp) Dijon mustard
125 g (4 oz) butter or margarine, softened
1 long, crusty, black rye loaf

1 Beat the garlic and mustard into the butter.

2 Thickly slice the rye loaf and spread the slices thinly with the butter and garlic mixture. Reshape the loaf and wrap in foil. Bake in the oven at 200°C (400°F) mark 6 for about 25 minutes. Serve while still warm.

*205 Calories per serving*

# CURRANT COMPOTE

*Serve this refreshing summer dessert with single cream and fresh home-made Madeleines (see page 72).*

225 g (8 oz) raspberries
150 g (5 oz) caster sugar
lemon juice
450 g (1 lb) red currants, stalks removed
single cream, to serve

1 Put the raspberries and sugar in a medium saucepan. Heat gently, stirring, for about 5 minutes or until the juice begins to run. Push through a nylon sieve, add lemon juice to taste and leave to cool.
2 Pile the currants into tall individual glasses or one pretty glass serving bowl. Pour the raspberry sauce over the currants. Chill for at least 1 hour before serving with single cream.

*190 Calories per serving*

*Currant Compote (above), Madeleines (page 72)*

# Madeleines

*Even the freshest of these tiny shell-like sponge cakes can seem slightly dry when eaten alone. To be truly appreciated, Madeleines must be served with a juicy fruit compote.*

150 g (5 oz) butter or margarine
white vegetable fat, melted
plain flour
3 eggs
150 g (5 oz) caster sugar
2.5 ml (½ level tsp) baking powder
salt
grated rind of 1 lemon

1 Melt the butter and leave to cool slightly. Brush a sheet of Madeleine moulds with melted white vegetable fat. Dust with flour, shaking off any excess.

2 Beat the eggs and sugar together until rich and creamy. Add 150 g (5 oz) flour, the baking powder, a pinch of salt and the lemon rind. Beat well. Pour in the melted butter and stir until blended.

3 Half-fill the moulds with the mixture and leave to stand for 10 minutes.

4 Bake in the oven at 220°C (425°F) mark 7 for about 12 minutes or until well risen and golden. Ease out of the tins and cool on a wire rack. Repeat until all the batter is used. Once cold, store Madeleines in polythene bags to help prevent them drying out. Serve as soon after making as possible.

MAKES ABOUT 24

*120 Calories per Madeleine*

# MIDDLE EASTERN DINNER PARTY

---

## Menu

*Grilled Goat's Cheese with Garden Salad* or a *Selection of Dips with Pitta Bread*

---

*Spiced Meat Skewers*
*Courgettes with Tomato*
*Pistachio Pilau*

---

*Peaches and Rose Cream*
*Almond Cigars*

SERVES 6

---

The cooking of the Middle East reflects the many influences of its rich and complicated history, and the wonderful, colourful variety of its people, from ancient times to the present. It has a tangled web of culinary traditions, sometimes simple, sometimes sophisticated, and – given the tradition of hospitality throughout the region – is ideal for partying. Middle Eastern people entertain easily and enthusiastically, using a wonderful mixture of ingredients and flavourings which are perfect for special-occasion meals.

To start the meal, offer a selection of Middle Eastern Dips with tiny bowls of olives and spiced nuts. Alternatively, if you prefer to serve a single dish, try our Grilled Goat's Cheese served with a Garden Salad.

The Spiced Meat Skewers, irresistibly flavoured with cumin and coriander, are served with a yogurt sauce, pistachio-flavoured rice and a delicious, cool courgette salad.

To finish, serve a delectable dessert of peaches and rosewater cream (or yogurt if preferred), splashed with strawberry sauce and accompanied by delicate nut-filled pastries.

--- **COUNTDOWN** ---

**The day before**

Wash the salad leaves for the starter, if serving the Goat's Cheese Salad. Make the dips, if serving, cover tightly and refrigerate. Slice the cheese into rounds. Store the cheese and salad leaves, covered, in the refrigerator. Make a vinaigrette dressing. Prepare and shape the mince mixture around skewers. Place on cling film-lined baking sheets. Cover loosely and refrigerate. Make the courgette and tomato dish, cover and refrigerate. Poach the peaches, drain and remove the stones – don't fill. Refrigerate, covered. Make the Almond Cigars.

**In the morning:**
Measure the rice. Peel the pistachio nuts. Prepare the ingredients for the yogurt sauce but do not mix. Make the strawberry sauce.

**To serve at 8 pm**
**About 6.30 pm:** Arrange the salad starters on individual plates or remove the dips from the refrigerator to allow them to come to room temperature. Cut out pitta breads and top with cheese. Mix the sauce for the kebabs. Cut a lemon. Assemble the peaches.
**7.30 pm:** Cook the rice and drain. Fry the nuts and keep the rice hot.
**7.45 pm:** Grill the kebabs, place in serving dishes and keep warm. Warm the pitta bread; grill the cheese toasts.

---

### FREEZER NOTES

*The Courgettes with Tomato can be frozen but will be more liquid on thawing. Pack and freeze the poached, peeled peaches in their cold syrup. Thaw for about 6 hours, then complete as directed. Freeze the Almond Cigars in a rigid container. When required, thaw for 3–4 hours before serving.*

---

# GRILLED GOAT'S CHEESE WITH GARDEN SALAD

*A hard, dry goat's cheese is best for this dish but if you find this hard to come by, use French Chèvre Blanc instead.*

275 g (10 oz), 7.5 cm (3 inch) round piece firm goat's cheese
small round or oval pitta breads
6 small handfuls garden lettuces (thinnings of ordinary lettuce, oakleaf, rocket, lamb's lettuce, chervil, etc.)
90 ml (6 tbsp) mild vinaigrette dressing
herb flowers

1 Slice the cheese across into six rounds, removing any hard rind. If necessary, trim the bread into 7.5–9 cm (3–3½ inch) rounds to fit under the cheese.
2 Top each circle of pitta with a piece of cheese. Grill under a high heat for 2–3 minutes or until just melted.
3 Serve each portion on a handful of salad dressed with vinaigrette and garnished with herb flowers. Accompany with extra warm pitta bread.

*385 Calories per serving*

---

*Spiced Meat Skewers (page 77), Pistachio Pilau (page 78), Courgettes with Tomato (page 78)*

# AUBERGINE CAVIAR

*In the Middle East, the aubergines for this dip are cooked on the barbecue rather than under the grill.*

2 large aubergines
3 garlic cloves, skinned and crushed
about 150 ml (¼ pint) tahina
juice of 3 lemons, or to taste
about 2.5 ml (½ level tsp) salt
black pepper

TO SERVE
coriander leaves
black olives
lemon wedges

1  Put the aubergines on the rack of a grill pan and grill under a moderate heat for 15–20 minutes, turning them constantly until the skin is black and blistered on all sides. Remove from the grill and leave until cool enough to handle. Carefully strip off the skin with your fingers.
2  Put the aubergine flesh in a blender or food processor with the garlic and work to a smooth purée. Add half the tahina and lemon juice and blend until smooth, then blend in the remaining tahina and lemon juice. Add the salt and a little pepper, taste and add more lemon juice and seasoning if liked.
3  Turn the purée into a serving bowl and smooth the surface. Cover the bowl and chill in the refrigerator until serving time.
4  To serve, uncover the bowl and garnish the caviar with coriander and olives. Serve lemon wedges separately. Serve with warm pitta bread.

*165 Calories per serving*

# TARAMASALATA

*This is a mild, creamy version of the popular smoked cod's roe dip.*

4 thick slices white bread, crusts removed
90 ml (6 tbsp) milk
125 g (4 oz) smoked cod's roe, skinned
2 garlic cloves, skinned and crushed
150 ml (¼ pint) olive oil
150 ml (¼ pint) groundnut or vegetable oil
75–90 ml (3–3½ fl oz) freshly squeezed lemon juice, or to taste
a few black olives, to garnish

1  Crumble the bread into a bowl, pour over the milk and leave to soak for 10 minutes. Squeeze the bread with your fingers to extract the liquid, then put the bread in a blender or food processor.
2  Break up the cod's roe and add to the machine with the garlic. Work these ingredients until well mixed. Mix the oils together and gradually add to the machine, blending well after each addition until smooth.
3  Blend in 75 ml (3 fl oz) lemon juice, then taste and add more lemon juice if liked. Blend in 30 ml (2 tbsp) hot water (this helps bind the mixture).
4  Turn the taramasalata into a serving bowl and swirl the surface with a palette knife. Cover and chill in the refrigerator until serving time.
5  To serve, uncover the bowl and garnish the taramasalata with olives. Serve with warm pitta bread.

*530 Calories per serving*

# Hummus bi Tahina

*Tahini is a paste made from sesame seeds. It can be bought in jars from health food shops, Greek or Cypriot grocers or large supermarkets.*

two 440 g (14.6 oz) cans chickpeas, drained and rinsed

3 garlic cloves, skinned and roughly chopped

150 ml (¼ pint) tahina

about 150 ml (¼ pint) lemon juice, or to taste

60 ml (4 tbsp) Greek-style natural yogurt

30 ml (2 tbsp) olive oil

salt and pepper

TO GARNISH

olive oil

paprika

chopped fresh parsley

1 Set a few whole chickpeas aside for the garnish, then work the remainder in a blender or food processor with the garlic, tahina and 90 ml (3½ fl oz) of the lemon juice until evenly mixed.

2 Add the yogurt, olive oil and salt and pepper to taste. Blend again until smooth, then add more lemon juice and season again. If the hummus is too thick, add more lemon juice according to taste.

3 Turn the purée into serving bowls and swirl the surface with a palette knife. Cover the bowls and chill in the refrigerator until serving time.

4 To serve, uncover the bowls and drizzle a little olive oil over the hummus. Arrange the reserved chickpeas in the centre of each bowl and sprinkle with paprika and parsley. Serve with warm pitta bread.

*385 Calories per serving*

# Spiced Meat Skewers

*Every region in the Middle East boasts a traditional 'kofta' recipe of minced lamb or beef mixed to a soft paste with spices and fresh herbs. For really successful, moist kebabs, use meat that is not too lean. Buy the skewers (satay sticks) from Chinese supermarkets.*

900 g (2 lb) minced beef or lamb

2 onions, skinned and grated

30 ml (2 level tbsp) ground cumin

15 ml (1 level tbsp) coarsely ground coriander

90 ml (6 level tbsp) finely chopped fresh parsley

salt and pepper

olive oil

paprika pepper

lemon wedges, to serve

FOR THE YOGURT SAUCE

3 spring onions

284 g (10 oz) carton natural yogurt

15 ml (1 level tbsp) chopped fresh mint

1 Get your butcher to mince the meat three times, or chop it in a food processor until very fine. Knead it with the grated onion, cumin, coriander, 60 ml (4 level tbsp) parsley and seasoning to make a smooth paste.

2 Take about 15–30 ml (1–2 level tbsp) of the mixture and press a flat sausage shape on to the ends of wooden skewers. Brush them lightly with oil and sprinkle with a little paprika.

3 Grill about half the kebabs at a time under a high heat for about 5 minutes. Turn, sprinkle with more paprika and grill the second side until well browned all over. (Keep the exposed wooden sticks away from the heat.)

4 Keep all the kebabs warm, loosely covered, until required. Sprinkle with parsley.

5 Meanwhile, make the sauce. Chop the spring onions, reserving a few dark green shreds for garnish, and mix with the yogurt and mint. Serve with the kebabs and lemon wedges.

*415 Calories per serving*

# COURGETTES WITH TOMATO

*Simple, cold vegetable dishes make a delicious accompaniment to grilled meat. Try courgettes with raisins, or aubergines with tomatoes and green peppers, or this sweet-sour sauce with courgettes and tomatoes.*

700 g (1½ lb) courgettes
salt and pepper
1 garlic clove, skinned and crushed
45 ml (3 tbsp) olive oil
350 g (12 oz) tomatoes
15–30 ml (1–2 tbsp) wine vinegar or cider vinegar
a pinch of sugar
chopped fresh parsley, to serve

1 Slice the courgettes into rounds about 1 cm (½ inch) thick. Sprinkle them lightly with salt and leave them to drain for 20 minutes. Pat dry.
2 Sauté the garlic in the oil for 30 seconds only, then add the courgettes and cook them gently on one side until almost tender. Turn and cook on the other side.
3 Meanwhile, skin and chop the tomatoes. Add to the pan with the vinegar, sugar and seasoning. Simmer until the vegetables are well done. Cool, then sprinkle with parsley to serve.

*110 Calories per serving*

# PISTACHIO PILAU

*This a highly decorative way of serving rice, perfect for a party. If pistachio nuts are not available, use chopped toasted almonds and chopped parsley to give a similar effect.*

oil
1 small onion, skinned and finely chopped
1 garlic clove, skinned and crushed
350 g (12 oz) long-grain rice
salt and pepper
50 g (2 oz) shelled pistachio nuts

1 Heat 30 ml (2 tbsp) oil in a frying pan and fry the onion and garlic for about 5 minutes or until the onion is beginning to soften but not colour. Stir in the rice and 500 ml (18 fl oz) lightly salted water. Bring to the boil, stirring once, then cover and simmer for about 20 minutes or until the rice is tender. Drain off any remaining water.
2 Meanwhile, peel the nuts and fry until golden in a little oil. Stir into the rice. Season to taste. Cover and keep warm until ready to turn out and serve.

*310 Calories per serving*

# PEACHES AND ROSE CREAM

*Triple-distilled rosewater, with its heady scent and taste, goes especially well with fresh peaches. Do try a bottle for this recipe and then add it to ice creams, custards and summer fruit dishes. It is available from pharmacists. The bottle we bought said 'for external use only' but we were assured by the chemist that small amounts can be used in cooking, though it must not be drunk neat.*

125 g (4 oz) granulated sugar
triple-distilled rosewater (see above)
6 ripe peaches, peeled and halved
225 g (8 oz) strawberries, hulled
150 ml (¼ pint) whipping cream, whipped, or thick natural yogurt

1 Put the sugar in a saucepan with 450 ml (¾ pint) water and heat gently until the sugar has dissolved. Bring to the boil, then reduce the heat and simmer for 5 minutes. Add 5 ml (1 tsp) rosewater and the peaches and cook very gently, covered, for 10–15 minutes, depending on their ripeness and size. Remove the peaches, cool them a little and remove the stones. Cool completely.
2 Meanwhile, purée the strawberries in a blender or food processor with 30–45 ml (2–3 tbsp) of the poaching syrup. Rub through a nylon sieve. Sandwich the peaches together or top each half with whipped cream or yogurt flavoured with rosewater. Place the peaches on individual plates and top with sauce.

*150 Calories per serving with yogurt*
*220 Calories per serving with cream*

# ALMOND CIGARS

*Paper-thin filo pastry can usually be found in the freezer cabinets of supermarkets or good delicatessens. (Take as many whole sheets of filo pastry as you need out of the packet and refreeze the rest.)*

125 g (4 oz) ground almonds
50 g (2 oz) caster sugar
a pinch of ground mixed spice
30 ml (2 tbsp) lemon juice
50 g (2 oz) butter
25 g (1 oz) polyunsaturated margarine
50 g (2 oz) filo pastry sheets
icing sugar for dusting

1 Mix together the almonds, caster sugar, mixed spice and lemon juice.
2 Melt the butter and margarine together. Cut the sheets of filo pastry into about twenty 12.5×7.5 cm (5×3 inch) oblongs. Stack them together in one pile and brush the top sheet with the melted butter and margarine.
3 Roll a small spoonful of almond filling into a log shape, then place along the shorter edge of the pastry. Roll the top sheet around this filling, making a cigar. Transfer to a greased baking sheet while buttering, filling and rolling the rest of the cigars. When all the pastries are completed, brush with any remaining butter.
4 Bake the rolls in the oven at 180°C (350°F) mark 4 for 15–20 minutes or until the pastries are crisp and golden. Cool and dust with icing sugar. Store in an airtight container.

MAKES ABOUT 20

*75 Calories each*

# An Exotic Feast

## Menu

*Fish with Lemon and Ginger*
*Green Beans with Cumin*
*Fragrant Saffron Pilau*
*Hot Spinach Dhal*
*Aubergine and Yogurt Relish*

*Kulfi*

SERVES 6

Although it's delicious, Indian food can be time-consuming to prepare. However, these simple recipes can be made well in advance and reheated at the last minute. There's no starter, but we've a selection of tasty main dishes and complementary accompaniments; all the recipes are suitable for non-meat-eaters. For dessert, try our wonderfully rich spiced ice cream called Kulfi.

## COUNTDOWN

**Well ahead**
Prepare the Kulfi to the end of step 5 and freeze.

**The day before**
Prepare and marinate the sole, cover and refrigerate overnight. Prepare and cook the Green Beans with Cumin. Cool, cover and refrigerate. Make the Fragrant Saffron Pilau, turn out into a bowl and cool. Place in a buttered ovenproof dish, cover with buttered foil and refrigerate. Make the Hot Spinach Dhal. Pour out into a bowl, cool, cover and refrigerate. Prepare the Aubergine and Yogurt Relish to the end of step 3. Cover and refrigerate. Chop the mint, cover and refrigerate separately.

**On the day**
Prepare the filling for the sole fillets, roll up and secure with cocktail sticks. Place on a plate, cover and refrigerate. Blend the coconut, saffron, cashew nuts and water for the fish sauce. Leave, covered, in a cool place (not the fridge).

Complete the Aubergine and Yogurt Relish. Cover and keep in the fridge.

**To serve at 8 pm**

**7 pm:** Take the rice out of the fridge. Preheat the oven to 180°C (350°F) mark 4. Place the Hot Spinach Dhal in a heavy-based pan with a large knob of butter, ready to reheat. Place the Green Beans with Cumin in a saucepan, ready to be reheated.

**7.15 pm:** Put the rice in the oven to reheat – allow 30–45 minutes, depending on the depth of the dish. Sauté the spring onions for the Fish with Lemon and Ginger, then complete the recipe, cover and leave to simmer.

**7.30 pm:** Transfer the Kulfi to the fridge to soften. Reheat the Dhal and the Green Beans, stirring frequently. Keep warm, covered, in a low oven.

**About 7.50 pm:** Add the cream to the Fish with Lemon and Ginger. Adjust the seasoning and garnish the dish.

**8 pm:** Serve the meal.

---

### FREEZER NOTES

*Only the Kulfi will freeze. Prepare to the end of step 5, cover and freeze for up to 1 month.*

---

# $F$ISH WITH LEMON AND GINGER

*This recipe has a lot of ingredients, but it's easy to make. Simmer gently to prevent the fish from breaking up. Alternatively, bring to the boil, cover and cook in the oven at 180°C (350°F) mark 4 for about 20 minutes or until the fish is tender.*

5 ml (1 level tsp) garam masala or good-quality curry powder
5 cm (2 inch) piece of fresh root ginger, peeled and finely chopped
2 garlic cloves, skinned and crushed
12 sole fillets, skinned, about 1.1 kg (2½ lb) total weight
175 g (6 oz) spring onions, chopped
45 ml (3 level tbsp) chopped fresh coriander
finely grated rind and juice of 1 lemon
salt and pepper
50 g (2 oz) creamed coconut
2.5 ml (½ level tsp) saffron strands
25 g (1 oz) salted cashew nuts
15 ml (1 tbsp) oil
142 ml (5 fl oz) carton single cream
chopped fresh coriander, salted cashew nuts and pared lemon or lime rind, to garnish

1 Mix together the garam masala, ginger and garlic. Place the sole fillets in a flat, non-metallic dish and rub over with the spice mixture. Cover tightly and marinate in the fridge overnight.

2 Mix half the spring onions with the coriander, lemon rind, 45 ml (3 tbsp) lemon juice and seasoning. Place the fillets, skinned-side up, on a plate and spoon a little of the onion mixture into the centre of each one. Roll up and secure with a cocktail stick.

3 In a food processor, blend the coconut, saffron and cashew nuts with 200 ml (7 fl oz) water.

4 Heat the oil in a large, shallow, flameproof casserole and sauté the remaining spring onions for 2–3 minutes. Add the coconut liquid and fish, with any remaining marinade. Bring to the boil, cover and simmer very gently for 15–20 minutes or until the fish is tender.

5 Add the cream and heat gently, without boiling, for a further 2–3 minutes. Adjust the seasoning and serve garnished with coriander, cashew nuts and lemon or lime rind.

*275 Calories per serving*

# GREEN BEANS WITH CUMIN

*These mildly spiced beans are perfect with the Fish with Lemon and Ginger.*

45 ml (3 tbsp) oil
125 g (4 oz) onions, skinned and sliced
700 g (1½ lb) green beans, topped and tailed, and halved if large
10 ml (2 level tsp) cumin seeds
450 g (1 lb) tomatoes, skinned and chopped
30 ml (2 level tbsp) tomato purée
salt and pepper

1 Heat the oil in a large sauté pan. Add the onions and cook, stirring, for 1–2 minutes. Add the beans and cumin seeds. Sauté, stirring, for a further 2–3 minutes.

2 Mix in the tomatoes, tomato purée, 150 ml (¼ pint) water and seasoning. Bring to the boil, cover and simmer for 15 minutes or until the beans are just tender. Adjust the seasoning before serving.

*80 Calories per serving*

*Left to right: poppadums, Fragrant Saffron Pilau (page 84), lassi yogurt drink, Green Beans with Cumin (above), Aubergine and Yogurt Relish (page 85), Fish with Lemon and Ginger (page 81), Hot Spinach Dhal (page 84)*

# Fragrant Saffron Pilau

*Fresh or dried morel mushrooms add a rich flavour to this pilau. Soak dried morels overnight and use some of the liquor to cook the rice.*

350 g (12 oz) basmati rice
60 ml (4 tbsp) oil
225 g (8 oz) button or morel mushrooms, sliced
3 cloves
6 green cardamom pods
1 stick cassia bark (see Cook's tip) or cinnamon
2.5 ml (½ level tsp) saffron strands
10 ml (2 level tsp) caster sugar
salt and pepper

1 Wash the rice in several changes of cold water. Place in a bowl, add 1 litre (1¾ pints) cold water and soak for 30 minutes. Drain and set aside.
2 Heat the oil in a large pan. Add the mushrooms, cloves, cardamom pods, cassia bark and rice. Stir over the heat for 1–2 minutes.
3 Add 600 ml (1 pint) cold water, the saffron, sugar and seasoning. Bring to the boil, stirring. Reduce the heat, cover tightly and cook very gently for about 15 minutes or until all the liquid is absorbed and the rice is tender.
4 Adjust the seasoning and fluff the rice with a fork before serving.

*280 Calories per serving*

## Cook's tip
*Cassia bark, available in Indian shops, has a slightly stronger flavour than cinnamon sticks. Use it sparingly.*

# Hot Spinach Dhal

*Simply omit or halve the chilli if you don't enjoy hot dishes. Use split moong dhal, washed moong beans, or red and green lentils.*

225 g (8 oz) moong dhal or lentils
75 g (3 oz) ghee (see Cook's tip) or butter
125 g (4 oz) onions, skinned and finely chopped
1 garlic clove, skinned and crushed
5 ml (1 level tsp) each ground coriander, ground turmeric and chilli powder
450 g (1 lb) frozen leaf spinach, thawed, drained and chopped
salt and pepper

1 Wash the dhal or lentils and leave to soak in cold water for 2 hours. Drain well.
2 Melt the ghee in a large sauté pan. Add the onion and garlic, and cook, stirring, for 2–3 minutes. Stir in all the remaining ingredients (except the spinach) with the dhal and cook, stirring, for 1–2 minutes.
3 Pour in 300 ml (½ pint) water with seasoning. Bring to the boil, cover and simmer for about 15 minutes or until the dhal is almost tender. Add a little more water if necessary.
4 Stir in the spinach and cook over a high heat, stirring, for 4–5 minutes or until thoroughly hot and all excess moisture has been driven off. Adjust the seasoning.

*230 Calories per serving*

## Cook's tip
*Ghee is clarified butter. It can be found in Indian shops. To make your own, melt unsalted butter until a foam forms on the top. Simmer for 1–2 minutes but do not let it brown. Cool slightly, then pour through a sieve lined with muslin or absorbent kitchen paper. Retain as much sediment as possible in the pan.*

# AUBERGINE AND YOGURT RELISH

*Fried aubergines absorb a lot of oil, so make sure you drain them well on absorbent kitchen paper before going on to complete the recipe.*

550 g (1¼ lb) aubergines, thinly sliced
salt and pepper
10 ml (2 level tsp) ground cumin
10 ml (2 level tsp) ground coriander
1.25 ml (¼ level tsp) chilli powder
about 150 ml (¼ pint) olive oil
142 g (5 oz) carton natural yogurt
1 garlic clove, skinned and crushed
15 ml (1 level tbsp) chopped fresh mint
sprig of fresh mint, to garnish

1  Place the aubergines in a colander and sprinkle liberally with salt. Leave to stand for 30 minutes, then rinse well and pat dry with absorbent kitchen paper. Mix together the cumin, coriander and chilli powder.

2  Heat a little of the oil in a large non-stick frying pan. Add enough aubergine slices to form a single layer and sprinkle with some of the spice mixture. Fry for 2–3 minutes or until golden brown and tender. Drain well on absorbent kitchen paper.

3  Repeat with the remaining slices, adding more oil as necessary. Leave to cool. Arrange the aubergine slices in a serving dish.

4  Mix together the yogurt, garlic, chopped mint and seasoning and spoon over the aubergines. Cover and chill in the fridge until required. Garnish with a sprig of mint.

*250 Calories per serving*

# KULFI

*This classic ice cream has only a little cream added, but it is enriched with reduced milk. If you have an ice-cream maker, churn the mixture without the pistachio nuts, stirring these in once the ice cream has thickened.*

1.7 litres (3 pints) milk
6 green cardamom pods
150 g (5 oz) granulated sugar
50 g (2 oz) ground almonds
25 g (1 oz) pistachio nuts
142 ml (5 fl oz) carton double cream
a few drops of rosewater
shredded pistachio nuts, to decorate

1  Put the milk in a large heavy-based saucepan. Add the cardamoms and bring to the boil. Simmer for about 1 hour or until the milk has reduced by half, stirring occasionally.

2  Stir the sugar into the milk, mixing well until dissolved. Strain the milk into a bowl and stir in the ground almonds. Leave to cool.

3  Meanwhile, cover the pistachio nuts with boiling water and leave for 1–2 minutes. Ease off the skins and then roughly chop or finely shred the nuts. Lightly whip the cream.

4  Stir the pistachio nuts and cream into the cold milk mixture with the rosewater.

5  Pour the mixture into a shallow freezerproof container and freeze for about 3 hours or until mushy. Beat lightly with a fork to break down the ice crystals. Freeze again for another hour or so, then beat lightly again. Spoon into individual ramekins (we used kulfi moulds from an Indian shop). Cover and freeze for 4–5 hours or until firm.

6  Leave to soften in the fridge for 1–1½ hours before serving decorated with shredded pistachio nuts.

*470 Calories per serving*

# DINNER BY CANDLELIGHT

## Menu

**Tomato and Cardamom Soup**
**Walnut Bread**

---

**Cinnamon Duck with Redcurrant Sauce**
**Roast Potatoes with Thyme**
**Carrot Purée**
**Spring Green Sauté**

---

**Pear Tart**

SERVES 6

---

Whether it's a birthday, anniversary or special get-together with friends, these recipes will make it a meal to remember. It starts with an unusual, bright tomato soup spiked with cardamom, served with delicious home-made Walnut Bread, if you have the time. This is followed by tender duck breasts which are roasted with cinnamon sticks until golden and crisp. The accompanying sauce, finished with red wine and redcurrant jelly, is deliciously sweet and aromatic.

To round off the dinner, we've suggested the lightest of pear tarts: a thin, crisp pastry base filled with ripe pear purée and topped with sliced fresh pears.

## COUNTDOWN

**The day before**
Prepare, blend and sieve the soup, then cool, cover and refrigerate. Make the Walnut Bread. Cool and wrap in foil. Make the sauce for the duck from step 3. Cool, cover and refrigerate. Prepare the carrot purée to the end of step 1, cover and refrigerate. Make the pastry case for the Pear Tart. Once cold, wrap in foil and store in a cool place. Prepare the pear purée, cover and refrigerate. Warm and sieve the apricot jam for the glaze. Place in a bowl, cover and store in a cool place.

**On the day**

**In the morning**

Shred the spring greens, place in a polythene bag and refrigerate. Peel the potatoes, leaving them whole. Cover with cold water and store in a cool place. Wash the watercress garnish for the duck and refrigerate in a polythene bag.

**To serve at 8 pm**

**About 6 pm:** Complete and glaze the Pear Tart. Leave in a cool place.

**6.15 pm:** Preheat the oven to 200°C (400°F) mark 6. Parboil the potatoes and put in the oven to roast.

**7 pm:** Brown the duck breasts and put in the oven to roast.

**About 7.40 pm:** Reheat the carrot purée, cover and keep warm. Reheat the soup and the duck sauce. Stir-fry and complete the spring greens, cover and keep warm. Check the duck and potatoes. Keep warm, uncovered. Put the bread in the oven to warm through for about 5 minutes. Cover with foil if your guests aren't ready.

**8 pm:** Serve the soup. Slice the duck just before serving, then spoon over a little sauce.

---

### FREEZER NOTES

*Prepare, blend and sieve the soup, pack and freeze. When required, thaw overnight at cool room temperature. Reheat to serve. Make the Walnut Bread, cool, overwrap and freeze for up to 1 week – no more or the crust will lift off. Thaw at room temperature, then refresh in the hot oven for 5 minutes before serving. Make the redcurrant sauce for the duck, pack and freeze. Thaw overnight at cool room temperature; reheat to serve. Prepare the carrot purée to the end of step 1, pack and freeze. Thaw overnight at cool room temperature; reheat to serve. Make and bake the pastry case for the Pear Tart; cool, pack in a rigid container and freeze. Thaw at cool room temperature for 2 hours.*

---

# $T$OMATO AND CARDAMOM SOUP

*If available, use large beef tomatoes – they give a really fine flavour.*

30 ml (2 tbsp) olive oil
175 g (6 oz) onions, skinned and roughly chopped
2 garlic cloves, skinned and crushed
275 g (10 oz) potatoes, peeled and roughly chopped
6 green cardamom pods, split
salt and pepper
15 ml (1 tbsp) lemon juice
900 g (2 lb) fresh ripe tomatoes, preferably beef tomatoes, roughly chopped
100 ml (4 fl oz) dry white wine
400 g (14 oz) can chopped tomatoes
450 ml (¾ pint) chicken stock
a small bunch fresh chives and parsley, to garnish
Walnut Bread, to serve (optional)

1 Heat the oil in a large saucepan and sauté the onions for 2–3 minutes. Add the garlic, potatoes, cardamoms, seasoning and the lemon juice. Cook, stirring, for 1–2 minutes.

2 Add all the remaining ingredients, except the chives and parsley. Bring to the boil, cover and simmer for 40 minutes or until the potatoes become very tender. Cool the mixture slightly.

3 Purée the soup in a blender or food processor with half the chives until smooth. Rinse out the saucepan and sieve the mixture back into the pan. Reheat to serve, whisking the soup until smooth. Garnish with the remaining herbs and serve with slices of warm Walnut Bread, if liked.

*120 Calories per serving*

# Walnut Bread

*Fast-action dried yeast, available from supermarkets, is an absolute boon for the busy cook. Only one kneading, rising and proving is necessary, and there is no messy mixing, as the dried yeast is stirred straight into the flour; the water is added afterwards. This recipe makes two loaves. One should be enough to serve with the starter; keep the other in the freezer for another meal.*

600 g (1 lb 5 oz) strong white flour
5 ml (1 level tsp) salt
25 g (1 oz) butter or margarine
1 sachet fast-action dried yeast
125 g (4 oz) shelled walnuts, roughly chopped
about 350 ml (12 fl oz) tepid water

1 Sift the flour and salt into a warmed large mixing bowl. Rub in the butter with your fingertips, then stir in the yeast and chopped walnuts.
2 Pour in enough tepid water to make a smooth dough, mixing with a wooden spoon, then form the mixture into a ball of dough with your hands.
3 Turn the dough out on to a floured surface and knead for 10 minutes or until smooth and elastic, adding a little more flour if the dough becomes too sticky.
4 Divide the dough in half and shape each piece into a roll. Place on oiled baking sheets, cover with a clean, damp cloth and leave to rise in a warm place for about 1 hour or until doubled in size.
5 Uncover the loaves and slash the tops with a knife. Bake in the oven at 220°C (425°F) mark 7 for 10 minutes. Reduce the oven temperature to 190°C (375°F) mark 5 and bake for a further 25 minutes or until the loaves are crusty on top and sound hollow when tapped on the bottom, swapping over oven shelves halfway through to ensure even cooking. If the loaves become too brown during baking, cover them with grease-proof paper or foil.
6 Leave the loaves to cool on a wire rack. Warm in the oven just before serving.

*260 Calories per serving*

---

❧

# Cinnamon Duck with Redcurrant Sauce

6 boneless duck breasts, about 175 g (6 oz) each
2 cinnamon sticks
15 ml (1 tbsp) olive oil
175 g (6 oz) onions, skinned and roughly chopped
1 garlic clove, skinned and crushed
300 ml (½ pint) chicken stock
300 ml (½ pint) red wine
5 ml (1 level tsp) dried marjoram
15 ml (1 level tbsp) Dijon mustard
1.25 ml (¼ level tsp) ground cinnamon
30 ml (2 level tbsp) redcurrant jelly
salt and pepper
watercress and fresh figs (optional), to garnish

1 Put two or three of the duck breasts, skin-side down, in a large, preferably non-stick, sauté pan with the cinnamon sticks. Fry until well browned, turning once. (There should be no need to add any fat to the pan.) Repeat with the remaining duck breasts.
2 Place all the duck breasts with any pan juices and the cinnamon sticks in a single layer in a large roasting tin. Cook in the oven at 200°C (400°F) mark 6 for 30 minutes or until crisp and golden and just cooked through.
3 Meanwhile, heat the olive oil in a medium saucepan and sauté the onion with the garlic until golden. Add all the remaining ingredients, except the watercress. Bring to the boil and bubble until reduced by about half. The

sauce should be syrupy. Strain and return to the rinsed-out saucepan to reheat.

4 Drain the duck well. Serve thickly sliced with a little of the sauce spooned over. Garnish with watercress and figs, if using. Serve the remaining sauce separately in a warmed sauceboat.

*370 Calories per serving*

# ROAST POTATOES WITH THYME

*Make sure you use plenty of thyme as it loses its strength during roasting.*

1.1 kg (2½ lb) old potatoes
salt and pepper
10 ml (2 level tsp) dried thyme
about 60 ml (4 tbsp) olive oil

1 Peel the potatoes and cut them into large chunks. Place in a saucepan, cover with cold, salted water and bring to the boil. Simmer for 1–2 minutes, then drain well.

2 Place the potatoes in a roasting tin and add the thyme, olive oil and seasoning. Mix well. Roast in the oven at 200°C (400°F) mark 6 for about 1¼ hours or until the potatoes become golden and crisp, turning occasionally and adding a little more oil if necessary. Keep warm, uncovered.

*230 Calories per serving*

# CARROT PURÉE

1.4 kg (3 lb) carrots, peeled and sliced
salt and pepper
40 g (1½ oz) butter
15–30 ml (1–2 tbsp) single cream (optional)
grated nutmeg (optional)

1 Cook the carrots in boiling salted water for about 30 minutes or until tender. Drain, then mash or blend in a food processor.

2 Return the purée to the saucepan with the butter, cream, if using, and seasoning, adding nutmeg to taste, if using. Reheat, stirring frequently, until the purée is hot and any excess moisture has evaporated. Spoon into a serving dish, sprinkle with nutmeg, if using, and keep warm, covered.

*110 Calories per serving*

# SPRING GREEN SAUTÉ

700 g (1½ lb) spring greens
30 ml (2 tbsp) olive oil
25 g (1 oz) butter
1 garlic clove, skinned and crushed
15 ml (1 tbsp) lemon juice
salt and pepper

1 Coarsely shred the spring greens, discarding any thick stalks. Rinse and drain.

2 Heat the oil and butter in a large wok or sauté pan. Add the spring greens and garlic and stir-fry over a high heat for 4–5 minutes or until just tender. Add the lemon juice and seasoning and keep warm in a covered dish.

*90 Calories per serving*

# $P$EAR TART

125 g (4 oz) butter
175 g (6 oz) plain flour
25 g (1 oz) caster sugar
1 egg yolk
7 medium firm, ripe, red-skinned pears, about
1.1 kg (2½ lb) total weight
30 ml (2 tbsp) Calvados or brandy
30 ml (2 tbsp) lemon juice
120 ml (8 level tbsp) apricot jam

1 First make the pastry. Rub the butter into the flour. Mix in the sugar and bind to a firm dough with the egg yolk mixed with 15 ml (1 tbsp) water. Knead lightly until just smooth.
2 Roll out the pastry on a lightly floured surface and use to line a 23 cm (9 inch) loose-based fluted flan tin. Bake blind in the oven at 200°C (400°F) mark 6 for 10–15 minutes or until the pastry is golden brown. Cool.
3 Meanwhile, set aside three of the best pears and peel, quarter and core the remainder. Place in a food processor with 15 ml (1 tbsp) each of the Calvados and lemon juice. Blend until smooth. Turn into a bowl, cover tightly and refrigerate until required.
4 Warm the jam with the remaining Calvados and lemon juice. Sieve and return to the pan.
5 Spoon the pear purée into the flan case. Thickly slice and core the remaining pears and scatter over the purée.
6 Reheat the glaze and then brush it carefully over the pears, spooning the remainder over the pear purée. Leave for 20–30 minutes to allow the glaze to set before serving.

*415 Calories per serving*

*Left to right: Cinnamon Duck with Redcurrant Sauce (page 88); Carrot Purée, Spring Green Sauté, Roast Potatoes with Thyme (page 89)*

# SOME ENCHANTED EVENING

## Menu

*Summer Platter*

---

*Duckling Salad with Ginger Dressing*
*Mixed Pepper Salad*
*Tabbouleh*
*Focaccia, Ciabatta or any Continental Bread*

---

*Sparkling Strawberries*
*Langues de Chat*

SERVES 6

Quick and easy to prepare, this delicious romantic supper is perfect for eating outdoors on a warm summer evening.

---

### COUNTDOWN

**The day before**
Cook the duckling for the duckling salad, cool and refrigerate. Wash the salad leaves and refrigerate in a polythene bag. Make the dressing and store in the refrigerator. Make the Mixed Pepper Salad, cool and refrigerate. Make the Tabbouleh. Make the Langues de Chat and store in an airtight container.

**On the day**
**In the morning**
Prepare the Summer Platter ingredients. Refrigerate. Hull the strawberries and chill.

**To serve at 8 pm**
**About 7 pm:** Remove all the ingredients, except the strawberries, from the fridge.
**7.30 pm:** Arrange the Summer Platter. Arrange the Duckling Salad.
**8 pm:** Serve the meal.

> **FREEZER NOTES**
> *Only the Langues de Chat biscuits can be frozen. Pack into rigid containers and freeze. Allow to thaw for 1 hour before serving.*

# SUMMER PLATTER

900 g (2 lb) small new potatoes
salt and pepper
900 g (2 lb) asparagus
12 large cooked prawns with shells
12 radishes
1 packet bread sticks
142 ml (5 fl oz) carton soured cream
15 ml (1 level tbsp) chopped fresh herbs
chives, to garnish
100 g (4 oz) jar black or red lumpfish caviar

1 Cook the potatoes in boiling salted water until just tender. Drain and leave to cool. Blanch the asparagus in boiling salted water until just cooked. Drain and refresh under cold water.
2 Arrange the potatoes, asparagus, prawns, radishes and bread sticks on a large platter. Serve with a small bowl of soured cream mixed with chopped fresh herbs and garnished with chives. Let guests help themselves to the lumpfish caviar. If time allows, cut the potatoes in half, spread each half with some soured cream and top with a little lumpfish caviar.

*285 Calories per serving*

## VARIATIONS

Place a small piece of smoked salmon on each half of potato before topping with the soured cream and caviar. Try adding chopped chives or spring onions to the soured cream. If you are counting calories, use fromage frais rather than soured cream.

# DUCKLING SALAD WITH GINGER DRESSING

6 boneless duckling breasts, 125 g (4 oz) each
salt and pepper
mixed salad leaves
toasted pine nuts and orange slices, to garnish

### FOR THE GINGER DRESSING
3 spring onions, finely chopped
100 ml (4 fl oz) olive oil
30 ml (2 tbsp) lemon juice
grated rind and juice of 1 orange
5 ml (1 level tsp) caster sugar
15 ml (1 level tbsp) peeled and grated fresh root ginger
1 garlic clove, skinned and crushed
10 ml (2 tsp) sesame oil
10 ml (2 tsp) soy sauce

1 Prick the duckling breasts all over with a sharp knife, then sprinkle with salt. Place the breasts, skin-side down, on a wire rack over a roasting tin. Cook in the oven at 200°C (400°F) mark 6 for 10 minutes. Turn and cook for 20 minutes or until tender and the skin is crisp. Cool, then slice thickly.
2 Tear the salad leaves into small pieces and arrange on a platter.
3 Combine all the dressing ingredients.
4 Toss the duckling with half the dressing and arrange on the salad. Garnish with pine nuts and orange. Serve with the remaining dressing.

*710 Calories per serving with skin*
*410 Calories per serving without skin*

# MIXED PEPPER SALAD

*We used red, yellow and orange peppers, as they are sweeter than green.*

30 ml (2 tbsp) Ginger Dressing (see Duckling
Salad, page 93)
8 medium peppers (mixture of red, yellow and
orange), de-seeded and sliced into thin strips
salt and pepper

1  Heat the dressing in a wok or frying pan. Add half the peppers and fry for 3–4 minutes or until slightly softened. Remove from the pan with a slotted spoon and drain on absorbent kitchen paper.

2  Fry the remaining peppers, adding a little more dressing if necessary. Drain as before and leave to cool. Serve warm or cold, without extra dressing.

*60 Calories per serving*

*Left to right: Summer Platter (page 93), Mixed Pepper Salad (above), Duckling Salad with Ginger Dressing (page 93)*

# Tabbouleh

225 g (8 oz) burghul
90 ml (6 tbsp) olive oil
90 ml (6 tbsp) lemon juice, or more to taste
about 4 garlic cloves, skinned and finely chopped
25 g (1 oz) fresh parsley, finely chopped
25 g (1 oz) fresh mint, finely chopped
salt and pepper
4 ripe tomatoes, skinned, seeded and chopped
1 bunch spring onions, finely chopped

1 Soak the burghul in 600 ml (1 pint) luke-warm water for 30 minutes.

2 Drain the burghul in a sieve, squeezing it with your hands to extract the water. Tip it out on to a clean tea-towel, gather the corners together and wring out the water so that the burghul is as dry as possible.

3 Whisk the oil and lemon juice together in a bowl with the garlic, herbs and salt and pepper to taste. Add the burghul and toss to coat in the dressing.

4 Add the tomatoes and spring onions and fork through until evenly distributed. Taste and adjust the seasoning, adding more lemon juice if you like. Serve at room temperature.

*285 Calories per serving*

# Langues de Chat

*This mixture makes a lot of biscuits but they're light and delicate and, if any are left over, will store well for several days.*

75 g (3 oz) butter or margarine, softened
75 g (3 oz) caster sugar
1 egg (size 1)
50 g (2 oz) plain flour
25 g (1 oz) ground almonds

1 Put all the ingredients in a mixing bowl and whisk together until evenly blended.

2 Spoon the mixture into a piping bag fitted with a 0.5–1 cm (¼–½ inch) plain nozzle. Pipe out into thin 5 cm (2 inch) lengths on baking sheets lined with non-stick baking parchment. (There should be about 48 biscuits.) Allow them plenty of room to spread – you'll need three or four baking sheets, or simply bake them in rotation, putting one batch in the oven as the last one is cooked.

3 Bake in the oven at 200°C (400°F) mark 6 for 6–7 minutes or until tinged with colour. Using a palette knife, immediately ease the biscuits off the paper and cool on wire racks. Store them in an airtight container until required.

MAKES ABOUT 48

*25 Calories per biscuit*

# Sparkling Strawberries

900 g (2 lb) strawberries, hulled
15 ml (1 level tbsp) icing sugar
300 ml (½ pint) champagne or sparkling white wine, well chilled
Langes de Chat and double cream, to serve

1 Rinse the strawberries, if wished, and place in a large bowl. Sprinkle over the icing sugar and mix gently so all the strawberries are covered. Cover and leave to chill. Remove the strawberries from the fridge about 30 minutes before serving to allow to come to room temperature.

2 Just before serving, pour over the champagne or sparkling wine and serve, accompanied by Langues de Chat and double cream.

*75 Calories per serving*

# SIMPLY SPLENDID

---

## Menu

### Salmon and Prawn Mousse

---

### Poached Pheasant with Apple and Pecan Nuts
### Creamed Potato and Celeriac
### Grilled Vegetables (Red Peppers, Onions, Mushrooms, Patty Pan Squash, Baby Corn)

---

### Chocolate Roulade

SERVES 6

---

The charm of this delicious dinner party lies in planning. Everything but the vegetables and salad garnish can be made the day before and quickly finished off just before serving. The Salmon and Prawn Mousse is a delicate, light start, followed by pheasant, a seasonal meat, which is now more readily available. We cooked accompanying vegetables as above, but you can use others, such as courgettes instead of patty pan squash. And chocoholics will love our rich Chocolate Roulade, which uses cocoa powder to flavour a moist sponge, rolled and filled with whipped cream. You'll be surprised at just how easily you can prepare this elegant meal.

## COUNTDOWN

**Two days before**
Marinate the pheasant breasts as in step 1.

**The day before**
Make the Salmon and Prawn Mousse, leave in the tin, cover and refrigerate. Complete the pheasant dish to the end of step 5. Cool, cover and refrigerate. Toast the pecans. Make the Creamed Potato and Celeriac to the end of step 2. Cool, cover and refrigerate. Make the Chocolate Roulade to the end of step 4, and the chocolate leaves, if using. Cover loosely and refrigerate. Refrigerate the leaves.

**On the day**

**To serve at 8 pm**

No earlier than 4 pm, prepare the salad garnish for the Salmon and Prawn Mousse. Refrigerate in polythene bags. Chop the watercress for the Creamed Potato and Celeriac. Cover and refrigerate. Prepare accompanying vegetables.

**6 pm:** Turn out and slice the Salmon and Prawn Mousse. Place on serving plates. Cover loosely with damp greaseproof paper and refrigerate.

**7.30 pm:** Bring the pheasant to the boil. Reheat for about 12 minutes. Caramelise the apples and pecans. Reheat the creamed potato with the butter, milk and watercress. Cook accompanying vegetables. Remove the mousse from the fridge.

**8 pm:** Remove the Chocolate Roulade from the fridge. Garnish the starter and serve.

---

**FREEZER NOTES**

*Do not freeze the mousse. Pack and freeze the pheasant dish at the end of step 5. To use, thaw overnight at cool room temperature, then complete as in the Countdown. Freeze the Chocolate Roulade at the end of step 4. Thaw in the fridge for 4 hours. Freeze the baked (unfilled) pastry case.*

*Poached Pheasant with Apple and Pecan Nuts (page 100), Creamed Potato and Celeriac (page 101), grilled vegetables*

Maxine

# Salmon and Prawn Mousse

350 g (12 oz) tail-end piece fresh salmon or sea trout

175 g (6 oz) frozen queen scallops, thawed

1 small carrot, peeled and sliced

2 bay leaves

peppercorns

salt and pepper

75 ml (5 tbsp) white wine

15 ml (1 level tbsp) powdered gelatine

300 ml (½ pint) milk

1 small onion, skinned and sliced

25 g (1 oz) butter

30 ml (2 level tbsp) plain flour

75 ml (5 level tbsp) mayonnaise

grated rind and juice of 1 lemon

150 ml (¼ pint) whipping cream

225 g (8 oz) cooked peeled prawns

1 egg white

shredded cucumber, to garnish

toasted olive bread, to serve

1 Cut the salmon into four steaks and place in a shallow pan. Add the scallops, carrot, a bay leaf, a few peppercorns and a pinch of salt. Spoon over the wine and 75 ml (5 tbsp) water. Bring slowly to the boil, then remove the scallops. Drain the scallops and pull off the tough, dark muscle and discard. Separate the orange coral from the white flesh. Cover and simmer the salmon for 10–15 minutes.

2 Flake the salmon, discarding the skin and bones. Bubble the pan juices to reduce by half. Strain and reserve.

3 Spoon 45 ml (3 tbsp) water into a small heat-proof bowl. Sprinkle over the gelatine and leave to soak.

4 Place the milk, onion, remaining bay leaf and a few peppercorns in a saucepan. Bring to the boil, then remove from the heat, cover and leave to infuse for 10 minutes. Strain. Melt the butter and stir in the flour and strained milk. Season, bring to the boil and bubble for 2–3 minutes or until thickened. Add the gelatine and stir until dissolved. Transfer to a larger bowl and leave to cool.

5 Stir the fish into the sauce with the reserved cooking juices and beat well. Fold in the mayonnaise, lemon rind, 30 ml (2 tbsp) lemon juice, the lightly whipped cream, scallops and prawns, and the lightly whisked egg white. Season. Line the base of a 1.3 litre (2¼ pint), 900 g (2 lb), non-stick loaf tin with foil. Spoon in the mousse mixture. Chill for about 3 hours or until set. Cover loosely.

6 Loosen around the edges of the mousse, then turn out on to a flat plate. Slice and place on individual serving plates. Allow 30 minutes at room temperature, then garnish and serve.

*450 Calories per serving*

# Poached Pheasant with Apple and Pecan Nuts

6 pheasant breasts/supremes, 125 g (4 oz) each

30 ml (2 tbsp) hazelnut oil, olive oil or walnut oil

unsalted butter

125 g (4 oz) carrots, peeled and finely chopped

125 g (4 oz) leeks, finely chopped

125 g (4 oz) onions, skinned and finely chopped

15 ml (1 level tbsp) plain flour

350 ml (12 fl oz) dry cider

300 ml (½ pint) stock

20 ml (4 level tsp) soft brown sugar

salt and pepper

3 Cox's Orange Pippin apples, quartered, cored and thickly sliced

50 g (2 oz) pecan nuts, toasted, or walnuts

1 Place the pheasant breasts in a bowl, pour over the oil and stir well. Cover and marinate in the fridge overnight.

2 Melt 50 g (2 oz) butter in a large, shallow flameproof casserole. Brown three pheasant breasts at a time, then remove from the pan.

3 Add the vegetables to the pan and sauté for 4–5 minutes or until golden brown. Stir in the flour, cider, stock, half the sugar and seasoning. Bring to the boil, stirring.

4 Return all the pheasant breasts to the pan, cover and simmer for 30-35 minutes until tender.

5 Remove the pheasant with a slotted spoon. Pour the vegetables and liquid into a food processor and blend until smooth. Strain into the rinsed-out casserole and add the pheasant.

6 Cover the casserole and simmer gently for 5–7 minutes. Melt 25 g (1 oz) butter in a pan and add the apple slices. Stir in the nuts and remaining sugar. Sauté for 2–3 minutes or until the mixture caramelises, stirring frequently. Spoon over the pheasant and serve.

*535 Calories per serving*

## CREAMED POTATO AND CELERIAC

900 g (2 lb) potatoes
450 g (1 lb) celeriac
salt and pepper
lemon juice
25 g (1 oz) butter
30 ml (2 tbsp) milk
30 ml (2 level tbsp) roughly chopped watercress

1 Peel the potatoes and celeriac and slice. Place in a large saucepan of cold, salted water acidulated with lemon juice. Bring to the boil, then reduce the heat, cover and simmer for 25–30 minutes or until tender.

2 Drain the vegetables and mash until smooth.

3 Return to a non-stick pan with the butter, milk and watercress. Reheat, stirring all the time. Season and serve.

*170 Calories per serving*

## CHOCOLATE ROULADE

60 ml (4 level tbsp) cocoa powder
150 ml (¼ pint) milk
4 eggs, separated
125 g (4 oz) caster sugar
225 ml (8 fl oz) double cream
chocolate leaves or grated chocolate, to decorate

1 Grease and line a 20.5×30.5 cm (8×12 inch) Swiss roll tin. Mix the cocoa powder and milk in a small saucepan and heat gently until the cocoa powder has dissolved. Remove the pan from the heat and set aside to cool.

2 Whisk the egg yolks and sugar together until pale and fluffy. Whisk the cooled milk mixture into the egg yolk mixture.

3 Whisk the egg whites until stiff, then fold into the cocoa mixture. Spread the mixture evenly in the prepared tin and bake in the oven at 180°C (350°F) mark 4 for about 20 minutes or until the sponge has risen and is just firm.

4 Turn out on to a sheet of greaseproof paper and cover with a warm, damp tea-towel to prevent the sponge drying out. Cool for 20 minutes.

5 Meanwhile, whip the cream until stiff. Spread over the sponge, reserving half for decorating, then roll the sponge up carefully. Do not roll it up too tightly and do not worry if it cracks slightly. Pipe the reserved cream on top and decorate with chocolate leaves or grated chocolate. Serve chilled.

*360 Calories per serving*

# PREPARE-AHEAD CHRISTMAS BUFFET

> ## Menu
>
> *Olives with Garlic and Lemon*
>
> ---
>
> *Spicy Lamb and Aubergines*
> *Carrot and Leek Galettes*
> *Mixed Leaf Salad*
>
> ---
>
> *Marsala Macaroon Parfait*
> *Lemon Ginger Cheesecake* or *Frozen Christmas Pudding*
>
> SERVES 12

Make Christmas entertaining a relaxed affair. This buffet for 12 can be prepared ahead, so your party should go off with the greatest of ease, while you're out there enjoying yourself along with your guests. To serve a bigger crowd, simply increase the quantities as required and add extra canapés from the selection given on pages 108–9.

The main course of Spicy Lamb and Aubergines has a Middle Eastern flavour with its mix of aubergines and spices. It can be topped with golden cheesy gnocchi or a scone-like cobbler topping.

---

## COUNTDOWN

**Up to two weeks ahead**
Prepare the Olives with Garlic and Lemon. Store in an airtight container and refrigerate. Make the Marsala Macaroon Parfait to the end of step 4. Make the Frozen Christmas Pudding, if serving.

**The day before**
Make the Spicy Lamb to the end of step 5. Cool, cover and refrigerate. Make the Carrot and Leek Galettes and place on baking sheets. Overwrap with foil and refrigerate. Make the

Lemon Ginger Cheesecake, if serving, but do not decorate. Cover and chill. Make the caramel shapes and store in an airtight container.

**On the day**
**To serve at 8 pm**
**In the morning:** Make a salad dressing and place in a screw-topped jar. Prepare the salad ingredients and store in polythene bags.
**6.45 pm:** Cook the Spicy Lamb as directed.
**7.30 pm:** Reheat the Carrot and Leek Galettes in foil at 200°C (400°F) mark 6 for 30 minutes. Open the foil for the final 15 minutes of heating.
**8 pm:** Stir the olives through the garlic and lemon dressing. Remove the Frozen Christmas Pudding from the freezer to soften, or decorate the cheesecake just before serving.

---

### FREEZER NOTES

*Cool, wrap and freeze the lamb dish at the end of step 5 before the final baking. To use, leave to thaw at cool room temperature for 12 hours. Refrigerate until cooking time, then bake until piping hot and the top is golden. To freeze the cobbler topping, open-freeze the rounds and double wrap. Use straight from the freezer. Place around the edge of the dish 20 minutes from the end of cooking time, brushed with a little milk. Freeze cooked and cooled Carrot and Leek Galettes on baking sheets; double wrap with foil. To use, thaw overnight at cool room temperature and reheat in the foil at 200°C (400°F) mark 6 for 30 minutes until piping hot. Open the foil after 15 minutes to allow excess steam to escape. Freeze the Parfait and Christmas Pudding as directed.*

---

# OLIVES WITH GARLIC AND LEMON

*These quick and easy nibbles are delicious with drinks. The olives can be stored, tightly covered, for two weeks in the fridge, if covered completely with olive oil. The flavoured oil can then be used for stir-frying, salad dressings and casseroles, etc.*

450 g (1 lb) mixed whole black and green olives
3 small red chillies
3 garlic cloves, skinned and sliced
30 ml (2 level tbsp) chopped fresh mixed herbs, such as thyme, marjoram, parsley, oregano
30 ml (2 level tbsp) citrus pepper
3 slices lemon, halved
150 ml (¼ pint) olive oil
cheese straws, to serve

1 Crack each olive with the end of a rolling pin, but do not crush. Crush the chillies between sheets of greaseproof paper.
2 Mix together the garlic, herbs, citrus pepper, crushed chillies, lemon slices and oil and pour over the olives. Stir well together.
3 Cover the olives and leave to marinate for at least 1 hour. Serve with warm cheese straws.

*150 Calories per serving*

# Spicy Lamb and Aubergines

*If you want to use the alternative Cobbler Topping (see right), omit step 1 of the recipe.*

olive oil

FOR THE GNOCCHI TOPPING
900 ml (1½ pints) milk
salt and pepper
1.25 ml (¼ level tsp) grated nutmeg
175 g (6 oz) semolina
125 g (4 oz) Parmesan cheese, grated
1 egg

900 g (2 lb) aubergines
4 red peppers
1.4 kg (3 lb) minced lamb
350 g (12 oz) onions, skinned and chopped
4 garlic cloves, skinned and chopped
2.5 ml (½ level tsp) ground allspice
30 ml (2 level tbsp) mild chilli seasoning
450 ml (¾ pint) dry white or red wine
45 ml (3 level tbsp) chopped fresh coriander
two 400 g (14 oz) cans chopped tomatoes
45 ml (3 level tbsp) tomato purée

1 Brush a Swiss roll tin with oil. Bring the milk to the boil with 7.5 ml (1½ level tsp) salt and the nutmeg. Turn down the heat and steadily pour in the semolina, stirring all the time. Simmer, stirring, for 2–3 minutes or until the mixture is very thick. Beat in the cheese and egg. Spread in the tin and level the surface. Cool and chill for 1 hour or until firm. Turn out and stamp out as many rounds as possible with a 5 cm (2 inch) round cutter. Cover and set aside.

2 Meanwhile, trim the ends off the aubergines and cut into ½–1 cm (¼–½ inch) rounds. Brush the cut sides lightly with oil and arrange on a grill pan. Grill for 3–4 minutes on each side or until golden brown. Arrange in overlapping cir-

cles in two 2.6 litre (4½ pint) ovenproof and freezerproof serving dishes.

3 Halve the red peppers, remove the seeds and place them, skin-side up, under a hot grill until well blackened and charred. Peel off the skin under cold water. Chop the peppers roughly.

4 Heat a frying pan and brown the meat in batches, adding a little oil if necessary. Transfer the meat to a large saucepan.

5 Brown the onions and garlic in residual oil. Add the allspice and chilli and cook for 1 minute. Stir into the lamb with the remaining ingredients and season well. Simmer, uncovered, for 1 hour or until well reduced and thick. Stir in the red peppers. Spoon the spicy lamb mixture over the aubergines. Arrange the rounds of gnocchi overlapping around the edges of the serving dishes.

6 Loosely cover with foil and bake in the oven at 200°C (400°F) mark 6 for about 1¼ hours or until golden brown and bubbling. Remove the foil 30 minutes before the end of the cooking time.

*420 Calories per serving (gnocchi topping)*
*525 Calories per serving (cobbler topping)*

# Cobbler Topping

450 g (1 lb) self-raising flour
2.5 ml (½ level tsp) salt
125 g (4 oz) Parmesan cheese, grated
125 g (4 oz) cold butter, diced
about 300 ml (½ pint) milk

1 Place the flour, salt and Parmesan in a bowl and rub in the butter.

2 Make a well in the centre and add enough milk to give a soft but manageable dough. Roll out to 1 cm (½ inch) thick. Stamp out 24 rounds with a 5 cm (2 inch) cutter. Place around the edge of the serving dishes 20 minutes before the end of the cooking time. Brush with milk and continue baking.

# CARROT AND LEEK GALETTES

*These are easily prepared ahead and reheated. We found a non-stick pan gave the best results.*

salt and pepper
900 g (2 lb) trimmed carrots, peeled and coarsely grated
900 g (2 lb) trimmed leeks, thinly sliced
1 egg, beaten
30 ml (2 tbsp) olive oil
50 g (2 oz) butter
fresh herbs, to garnish

1 Bring a large saucepan of salted water to the boil. Blanch the carrots and leeks together for 2 minutes. Drain well. Refresh under cold water and squeeze out excess moisture. Loosen the mixture with your fingers. Beat in the egg and season well.

2 Heat 15 ml (1 tbsp) oil in a 23 cm (9 inch) heavy-based frying pan. Add 25 g (1 oz) butter, and, when foaming, add half the mixture and press down well. Cook over a medium to low heat for 10 minutes or until the underside is golden and crisp. Loosen the galette around the sides. If the mixture is dry, add a little oil around the edges of the pan.

3 Invert a plate over the frying pan and turn upside-down, turning the galette on to the plate. Slide the galette back into the pan and continue to cook over moderate heat for 5 minutes. Repeat with the remaining mixture to make another galette, keeping the first warm. Serve in wedges garnished with fresh herbs.

*90 Calories per serving*

# MARSALA MACAROON PARFAIT

*This ice cream needs no special equipment or constant stirring – just make and freeze.*

1 vanilla pod or 7.5 ml (1½ tsp) vanilla essence
225 g (8 oz) caster sugar
6 egg yolks
50 ml (2 fl oz) Marsala
284 ml (10 fl oz) carton double cream
150 ml (5 fl oz) Greek-style natural yogurt
75 g (3 oz) ratafia, amaretti or macaroon biscuits, crushed
small biscuits, to serve

1 Soak the vanilla pod in a little warm water for 5 minutes to soften. Split and scrape out the seeds into a saucepan. Add the sugar and 100 ml (4 fl oz) water. Heat gently until the sugar dissolves. Turn up the heat and boil rapidly for 2–3 minutes.

2 Working quickly, beat the egg yolks with the Marsala, then pour the syrup on to the yolks in a steady stream, whisking all the time. Continue whisking for 6–8 minutes or until the mixture has doubled and is thick and foamy. Leave to cool slightly.

3 Whip the cream until it just holds its shape. Gently fold into the yolk mixture with the yogurt and the crushed ratafia biscuits. Spoon or pour into a freezer container and freeze for 3–4 hours or until firm.

4 Line two baking sheets with foil and place in the freezer to chill. Working quickly, scoop the parfait into balls and place on the chilled baking sheets. Cover and place in the freezer to refreeze.

5 To serve, chill a serving dish, pile the parfait balls into it and serve immediately, accompanied by small biscuits.

*260 Calories per serving*

# *L*EMON GINGER CHEESECAKE

*This smooth, creamy cheesecake is best if refrigerated overnight.*

125 g (4 oz) digestive biscuits, finely crushed
25 g (1 oz) stem ginger, finely chopped
50 g (2 oz) butter, melted
225 g (8 oz) full-fat soft cheese
397 g (14 oz) can condensed milk
175 ml (6 fl oz) lemon juice
whipped cream and caramel shapes
(see Cook's tip on page 53), to decorate

1  Line the base and sides of a 20.5 cm (8 inch) spring-release cake tin with non-stick baking parchment.
2  Mix the biscuits and ginger with the melted butter. Press into the prepared cake tin and chill in the fridge for about 30 minutes or until set.
3  In a food processor, blend the cheese and the condensed milk until smooth. Gradually drizzle in the lemon juice and continue blending for a further 2 minutes.
4  Pour the mixture over the set base, cover and return to the fridge for at least 3 hours, preferably overnight, or until set.
5  Remove from the tin and decorate with whipped cream and caramel shapes (see page 53) just before serving.

*445 Calories per serving*

*Left to right: mixed leaf salad, Carrot and Leek Galette (page 105), Olives with Garlic and Lemon (page 103), Spicy Lamb and Aubergines (page 104)*

# *F*ROZEN CHRISTMAS PUDDING

*This version is lighter than a traditional Christmas pudding but it has all the flavour.*

50 g (2 oz) no-soak dried apricots
175 g (6 oz) mixed currants, raisins and sultanas
finely grated rind of 1 orange
finely grated rind of 1 lemon
60 ml (4 tbsp) rum or brandy
5 ml (1 level tsp) ground mixed spice
284 ml (10 fl oz) carton double cream
500 g (1 lb 2 oz) carton or can ready-to-serve custard
75 g (3 oz) caster sugar
brandy, to serve (optional)

1 Snip the apricots into small pieces. In a large bowl, mix the apricots with the remaining dried fruit. Add the orange and lemon rinds, the rum and mixed spice. Cover and leave to soak for about 15 minutes – longer if possible.
2 Whisk the cream until it just holds its shape and fold it into the fruit with the custard and sugar.
3 Pour the mixture into an airtight container, cover and freeze for about 2 hours. Stir gently to distribute the fruits and break down any ice crystals. Re-cover, then freeze for about 6 hours or until firm.
4 To serve, remove from the freezer and leave at room temperature for about 15 minutes. Serve in scoops with a little extra brandy poured over if wished.

*340 Calories per serving*

# TIME-SAVING CANAPÉS

A party isn't a party without canapés. Serve about eight 'bites' per person, and leave the rest in the freezer for the next occasion.

## WHOLEWHEAT BLINIS

In a warm bowl, mix 125 g (4 oz) each plain wholewheat and plain white flour with 7 g (¼ oz) sachet fast-action dried yeast with 5 ml (1 level tsp) salt. Beat in 375 ml (13 fl oz) tepid milk, 1 large egg and 1 egg yolk until blended. Cover and leave to rise in a warm place for 1 hour. Fold in one softly whisked egg white and cook small spoonfuls of batter on an oiled griddle or frying pan, turning once. Cool and pack into a box. Freeze. Thaw at room temperature for 2 hours and serve warm or cold, topped with soured cream, lumpfish roe, chopped pickled herring or smoked salmon. Decorate with snipped fresh chives.

MAKES ABOUT 100

*40 Calories each*

## MINI CROISSANTS

Unroll one 240 g (8½ oz) can of Kool French Experience mini-croissant dough (available in chiller cabinets of most large supermarkets). Separate into triangles and cut each in half lengthways. Roll into croissants. Place on a baking sheet, brush with beaten egg and bake in the oven at 200°C (400°F) mark 6 for 8–10 minutes. Open-freeze, then pack into boxes. Thaw for about 1 hour at cool room temperature. Warm in a hot oven. Split and fill the croissants with soft cheese, smoked salmon or gravad lax and mustard.

MAKES ABOUT 48

*50 Calories each*

*Note: Alternatively, roll 7.5 cm (3 inch) triangles of puff pastry into croissants and bake as above.*

## ORIENTAL PARCELS

Cut 225 g (8 oz) filo pastry into 5×30.5 cm (2×12 inch) strips. Cover with a damp cloth. Mix four chopped spring onions with 225 g (8 oz) chopped cooked prawns, 30 ml (2 tbsp) light soy sauce, 5 ml (1 level tsp) grated fresh ginger and 1.25 ml (¼ level tsp) garlic salt. Spread a pastry strip with melted butter. Place about 2.5 ml (½ level tsp) of filling at the end of the strip and fold diagonally into a triangle. Continue folding to the end of the strip. Place on a greased baking sheet, brush with melted butter and sprinkle with sesame seeds. Prepare all the parcels similarly. Open-freeze, then pack carefully in rigid boxes. Bake from frozen in the oven at 220°C (425°F) mark 7 for 12–15 minutes or until crisp and golden. Serve warm.

MAKES ABOUT 60

*20 Calories each*

## BRUSCHETTA

Cut a thin French stick into 0.5 cm (¼ inch) slices. Place on a baking sheet and bake in the oven at 180°C (350°F) mark 4 for 10–15 minutes or until golden. Rub the slices with cut cloves of garlic and brush with olive oil. Cool and freeze. To serve, reheat in a hot oven for 2–3 minutes. Top with chopped pitted black olives and chopped canned pimentos or chopped fresh tomatoes. Garnish with herbs or finely chopped spring onion tops.

MAKES ABOUT 50

*35 Calories each*

## MINI PIZZAS

Stamp out 4 cm (1½ inch) rounds from two 20 cm (8 inch), 150 g (5 oz), ready-to-cook pizza bases. Top each with a slice of tomato, chopped spring onions and crumbled feta cheese. Freeze uncooked. Bake from frozen in the oven at 220°C (425°F) mark 7 for 8–10 minutes or until brown and bubbling.

MAKES ABOUT 40

*25 Calories each*

# CHRISTMAS DINNER PARTY

---

## Menu

*Christmas Mulled Wine*
*Blue Brie Toasts*
*Spiced Cashews*

---

*Marinated Salmon en Croûte with Orange Butter Sauce*
*Sesame Pilaff with Fennel*
*Mange-Touts with Cucumber*
*Mixed Green Salad*

---

*Fresh Pear Mousse with Caramelised Clementines*

SERVES 8

---

Extend a warming welcome to your guests when they arrive with our delicious Christmas Mulled Wine. Serve with Blue Brie Toasts and Spiced Cashews.

For a change from rich meats, we suggest a glorious fillet of salmon cooked en croûte. It's not as tricky as it sounds but never fails to impress – any leftovers are equally delicious served cold with mayonnaise and salad. The main course is complemented by our light Fresh Pear Mousse which could be served on its own or with Caramelised Clementines.

## COUNTDOWN

**About two days ahead**
Prepare the Blue Brie Toasts to the end of step 2, cover and refrigerate. Make the Spiced Cashews, leave to cool, then store in an airtight container.

**The day before**
Cook the Sesame Pilaff. Don't add the fennel tops yet. Cover and refrigerate. Make the Pear Mousse and the Caramelised Clementines and refrigerate.

110

**On the day**
**To serve at 8 pm**
**In the morning**
Make the Salmon en Croûte to the end of step 4. Cover tightly with cling film, cover and refrigerate. Prepare the green salad ingredients and store in polythene bags. Make a salad dressing.

**7.15 pm:** Cook the salmon as directed. Prepare the ingredients for the sauce. Reheat the pilaff in a buttered dish, topped with knobs of butter and tightly covered with foil. Add the fennel tops just before serving.

**7.45 pm:** Cook the Brie Toasts. Make the Mulled Wine.

**8 pm:** Serve the meal. While your guests are having drinks, finish the sauce and stir-fry the vegetables.

---

### FREEZER NOTES
*The recipes in this menu are not suitable for freezing.*

---

# CHRISTMAS MULLED WINE

3 small apples, studded with cloves
pared rind of 1 lemon
about 1.7 litres (3 pints) red wine
225 g (8 oz) brown sugar
3 cinnamon sticks
300 ml (½ pint) brandy

1 Put the clove-studded apples in a saucepan with the lemon rind, wine, sugar and cinnamon.
2 Bring to simmering point and simmer gently, covered, for 2–4 minutes.
3 Remove from the heat and add the brandy. Serve at once.

*355 Calories per serving*

# BLUE BRIE TOASTS

*These toasts can be prepared ahead, covered and refrigerated until you're ready to bake them.*

175 g (6 oz) blue brie cheese, rind removed
25 ml (1½ tbsp) mayonnaise
salt and pepper
5 thick slices crustless bread
butter for spreading

1 Beat together the cheese, mayonnaise and seasoning.
2 Spread one side of each slice of bread with butter, the other with the cheese and mayonnaise mixture, and cut into triangles.
3 Place the bread, buttered-side down, on baking sheets and bake in the oven at 200°C (400°F) mark 6 for 12 minutes or until crisp and brown underneath. Serve hot.

MAKES ABOUT 30

*45 Calories each*

---

# SPICED CASHEWS

275 g (10 oz) unsalted cashew nuts
25 g (1 oz) butter, melted
2.5 ml (½ level tsp) salt
10 ml (2 tsp) soy sauce
a few drops of Tabasco

1 Mix together all the ingredients in a medium bowl. Spoon evenly on to edged baking sheets.
2 Bake in the oven at 150°C (300°F) mark 2 for 15–20 minutes, stirring halfway through. Cool. Store in an airtight container for up to 2 weeks.

*220 Calories per serving*

# Marinated Salmon en Croûte

*Orange with salmon may sound unusual, but it is a wonderful partnership. This dish is also excellent served cold, accompanied by mayonnaise and a selection of fresh salads. If you're hesitant to tackle it yourself, ask your fishmonger to skin and fillet the fish for you, making sure you allow for the weight difference.*

1.6–1.8 kg (3½–4 lb) salmon or sea trout, cleaned, skinned and filleted (about 900 g/2 lb filleted weight)

coarsely grated rind and juice of 1 orange

5 ml (1 level tsp) coarsely ground black pepper

15 ml (1 level tbsp) chopped fresh dill or 10 ml (2 level tsp) dried dill weed

plain flour

700 g (1½ lb) ready-made puff pastry

350 g (12 oz) frozen chopped spinach, thawed

125 g (4 oz) low-fat soft cheese

salt and pepper

25 g (1 oz) butter or margarine

125 g (4 oz) spring onions, roughly chopped

125 g (4 oz) cooked peeled prawns

125 g (4 oz) small scallops

1 egg, beaten

fresh dill, slices of starfruit or orange, to garnish

Orange Butter Sauce, to serve

1 Sandwich the two salmon fillets together and place in a non-metallic dish. Mix together 45 ml (3 tbsp) orange juice with the coarsely ground pepper and the fresh dill. Rub the mixture into the salmon flesh. Cover with cling film, then leave to marinate for at least 1 hour.
2 On a lightly floured surface, roll out half the pastry thinly to a rectangle measuring 38×20.5 cm (15×8 inches). Place on a large baking sheet and prick all over with a fork. Bake in the oven at 200°C (400°F) mark 6 for about 15 minutes or until golden brown and cooked through. Leave to cool on a wire rack.

3 Squeeze all the excess liquid from the thawed spinach. Beat into the soft cheese and season. Melt the butter in a small saucepan and sauté the spring onions for 3–4 minutes or until just beginning to soften. Cool, then stir in the prawns, scallops and orange rind. Season.
4 Return the cooked pastry to a baking sheet and place one fish fillet on top, skin-side down. Trim the pastry, allowing 1 cm (½ inch) all round. Spread the spinach mixture over the fish. Spoon the prawn filling on top and finish with the remaining fillet, skin-side up.
5 Brush the cooked pastry edge with beaten egg, roll out the remaining pastry thinly and place over the fish to enclose completely. Trim off most of the excess pastry and reserve, leaving about 2.5 cm (1 inch) to tuck under all round. Decorate with a fine lattice of thin pastry strips cut from the trimmings and brush all over with beaten egg to glaze. Make two small holes in the pastry to allow steam to escape. Bake in the oven at 200°C (400°F) mark 6 for 40–45 minutes. The pastry should be well risen and golden brown. Serve warm on a bed of fresh dill. Garnish with slices of starfruit or orange and accompany with Orange Butter Sauce.

*625 Calories per serving*

# Orange Butter Sauce

*This zesty sauce cannot be made before the day as it tends to curdle on reheating.*

a few strands of saffron

5 egg yolks

grated rind and juice of 1 orange

1 garlic clove, skinned and crushed (optional)

225 g (8 oz) butter

salt and pepper

1 Grind the saffron strands to a powder with a pestle and mortar, or use a strong bowl and the end of a rolling pin. Place the egg yolks in a medium bowl and stir in the orange rind and 60 ml (4 tbsp) orange juice, the saffron strands and the garlic, if using.

2 Place the bowl over a pan half filled with water. Bring the water to a slow simmer. (Be careful not to let the water boil or the sauce will curdle.) Stir the egg mixture continuously, using a wooden spoon, for 2–3 minutes or until the mixture begins to thicken slightly.

3 Cut the butter into small dice and gradually beat it into the warm egg. The sauce will thicken slowly as the butter is added. Season to taste. Keep the orange mixture warm over the *slowly* simmering water until it is time to serve.

*245 Calories per serving*

---

# Sesame Pilaff with Fennel

*If Florence fennel is not available, use only 1.1 litres (2 pints) stock and stir in 30 ml (2 level tbsp) chopped fresh parsley or spring onion tops just before serving. It's important to use one of the suggested varieties of rice as it soaks up the liquid, becoming plump and tender rather than mushy.*

60 ml (4 level tbsp) sesame seeds
175 g (6 oz) Florence fennel, if available
50 g (2 oz) butter or margarine
125 g (4 oz) onion, skinned and finely chopped
125 g (4 oz) green pepper, de-seeded and finely chopped
a pinch of ground turmeric
350 g (12 oz) arborio, Carolina or pudding rice
about 1.3 litres (2¼ pints) chicken or vegetable stock
salt and pepper

1 Toast the sesame seeds under a hot grill until golden brown. Cool. If using Florence fennel, trim and finely chop the bulb, reserving the feathery tops. Finely chop and reserve the tops.

2 Melt the butter in a medium saucepan and sauté the onion, pepper and fennel with the turmeric for 2–3 minutes or until beginning to soften. Stir in the rice and continue to cook, stirring, for 1 minute before adding the stock, toasted sesame seeds and seasoning.

3 Bring to the boil, cover and simmer very slowly for about 45 minutes or until all the liquid is absorbed and the rice tender. Adjust the seasoning and stir in the reserved chopped fennel tops just before serving.

*255 Calories per serving*

## VEGETABLE VARIATIONS

A crisp, fresh green salad is ideal to accompany the salmon, and for an additional vegetable dish, make up a bowl of crunchy mange-touts and cucumber. You'll need 700 g (1½ lb) mange-touts and 1 large cucumber, and 30 ml (2 level tbsp) pine nuts. Slice the cucumber; blanch the mange-touts and cool. Stir-fry the cucumber and nuts in butter for 2 minutes, add the mange-touts and stir-fry for a further 1 minute before serving.

---

*Overleaf (left to right): Marinated Salmon en Croûte (page 112), mixed green salad, Orange Butter Sauce (page 112), mange-touts with cucumber (page 113), Sesame Pilaff with Fennel (page 113)*

# Fresh Pear Mousse

oil
25 ml (5 level tsp) powdered gelatine
300 ml (½ pint) milk
vanilla pod
3 egg yolks
45 ml (3 level tbsp) light muscovado sugar
900 g (2 lb ) ripe dessert pears
30 ml (2 tbsp) Poire Williams liqueur or Kirsch
284 ml (10 fl oz) carton double cream

1  Lightly oil a 1.4 litre (2½ pint) ring mould. Turn upside-down and drain on paper. Alternatively, lightly oil and base-line a 1.4 litre (2½ pint) soufflé dish with greaseproof paper. Sprinkle the gelatine over 75 ml (5 tbsp) water and leave to soak for 5 minutes.
2  Bring the milk and vanilla pod to the boil. Off the heat, add the soaked gelatine and stir until dissolved. Cover and leave to infuse for 5 minutes.
3  Whisk together the egg yolks and sugar until pale and thick. Strain over the hot milk, stirring until well blended.
4  Peel, quarter and core the pears. Purée with the egg custard and liqueur until smooth. Chill until just starting to set.
5  Whip the cream until it just begins to hold its shape and fold gently into the pear mixture. Pour into the prepared mould or soufflé dish and chill overnight.
6  To serve, dip the dish quickly into hot water and then invert on to a flat serving plate. Remove the lining paper and serve accompanied by Caramelised Clementines.

*290 Calories per serving*

# Caramelised Clementines

75 g (3 oz) granulated sugar
45 ml (3 tbsp) lemon juice
50 g (2 oz) shelled pistachio nuts
900 g (2 lb) clementines – or other 'easy-peelers'

1  In a large saucepan, dissolve the sugar over a low heat until it is a rich golden brown. Off the heat, add 600 ml (1 pint) water and the lemon juice. Bring to the boil, stirring. Simmer for 2–3 minutes, then leave to cool.
2  Blanch the nuts and remove the skins.
3  Peel the clementines and remove all the pith. Stir the fruit into the cold caramel syrup with the nuts. Cover and chill overnight.

*115 Calories per serving*

# AN ALTERNATIVE CHRISTMAS DINNER

## Menu

*Pizzettas*

---

*Rolled Plaice with Smoked Salmon*
*Light Leek Sauce*
*Crisp Vegetable Bake*
*Steamed Cauliflower with Artichoke Hearts and Black Olives*

---

*Glazed Lemon Puddings with Warm Cream Sauce*

SERVES 6

All the dishes in this simple menu are quick to prepare and temptingly light – perfect before and after all the over-indulgence at Christmas! Our Pizzettas are quicker to make and have fewer calories than traditional pizzas, while the Rolled Plaice with Smoked Salmon looks and tastes quite delicious. The additional vegetable dish of cauliflower steamed with artichokes is a tempting combination, but can be omitted from the menu. The refreshing Glazed Lemon Puddings finish off this meal perfectly.

---
### COUNTDOWN
---

**The day before**
Make the Light Leek Sauce to the end of step 2.

Cool, cover and refrigerate. Prepare the potatoes, cabbage and carrots for the Crisp Vegetable Bake to the end of step 3. Cool, pack in polythene bags and refrigerate. Prepare the spring onion and butter mixture for the Pizzettas, cover and refrigerate. Slice the tomatoes and courgettes. Place on a flat plate, cover and refrigerate. Prepare the cauliflower, if using, and refrigerate.

**On the day**
**In the morning**
Cut out the pastry circles for the Pizzettas, cover and refrigerate. Prepare the plaice to the end of step 2, cover and refrigerate. Make the sauce for the Glazed Lemon Puddings, cool, cover and refrigerate.

**To serve at 8 pm**

**6 pm:** Preheat the oven to 180°C (350°F) mark 4. Make the Glazed Lemon Puddings to the end of step 2. Set aside in a cool place.

**6.45 pm:** Prepare the fruits for the Glazed Lemon Puddings, cover and refrigerate. Raise the oven temperature to 230°C (450°F) mark 8.

**7.15 pm:** Cook the vegetable bake, cover loosely and keep warm, if necessary.

**7.30 pm:** Complete and bake the batch of Pizzettas.

**7.50 pm:** Cook the Rolled Plaice with Smoked Salmon. Gently reheat the Light Leek Sauce with the cooking liquor. Steam the cauliflower with artichoke hearts, if using, then stir in the black olives just before serving.

**8 pm:** Serve the meal. Gently warm the sauce for the Glazed Lemon Puddings and complete step 4 just before serving.

---

FREEZER NOTES

*The recipes in this menu are not suitable for freezing.*

---

*Left to right: Rolled Plaice with Smoked Salmon (page 120), cauliflower with artichoke hearts and black olives, Crisp Vegetable Bake (page 121), Light Leek Sauce (page 121)*

# Pizzettas

*Look out for frozen ready-rolled puff-pastry sheets in your supermarket. You can also make this recipe using a 375 g (13 oz) block of puff pastry. Roll it out to 0.5 cm (¼ inch) thick and cut out as directed.*

three 20.5 cm (8 inch) sheets frozen ready-rolled
puff pastry, thawed
3 spring onions, finely chopped
25 g (1 oz) butter, melted
grated rind and juice of 1 lemon
salt and pepper
30 ml (2 level tbsp) pesto sauce
350 g (12 oz) medium tomatoes, thinly sliced
225 g (8 oz) courgettes, thinly sliced
freshly grated Parmesan cheese, to serve

1 Cut out six 11 cm (4½ inch) rounds of pastry and place on an edged baking tray. Prick all over with a fork. Bake in the oven at 230°C (450°F) mark 8 for about 8 minutes or until lightly risen and golden.

2 Meanwhile, stir the spring onions into the butter, together with the grated lemon rind and 15 ml (1 tbsp) lemon juice. Season well.

3 Remove the pastry circles from the oven (they may have puffed up quite a bit) and spread each pastry circle with about 5 ml (1 level tsp) pesto sauce. Arrange slices of tomato and courgette, overlapping, on top of each circle and season well. Brush with the melted butter mixture.

4 Return to the oven for 10–12 minutes or until the tomatoes and courgettes have softened and the edges of the pastry are puffed and golden brown. Serve immediately, sprinkled with freshly grated Parmesan cheese.

*320 Calories per serving*

# Rolled Plaice with Smoked Salmon

*Ask the fishmonger to skin the plaice fillets for you. Smoked salmon trout works just as well as salmon.*

6 large plaice fillets, about 125 g (4 oz) each,
skinned
125 g (4 oz) smoked salmon
juice of 1 lemon
black pepper
100 ml (4 fl oz) dry white wine
Light Leek Sauce, to serve

1 Cut the plaice fillets in half lengthways. Cut the smoked salmon into strips approximately the same size as the plaice.

2 Lay the plaice on a board, skinned-side up, and place a strip of salmon on top, patching with more salmon, if necessary. Squeeze a little lemon juice over each portion and grind over plenty of black pepper. Roll up each fillet carefully.

3 Pour the wine into a flameproof casserole and add the rolls of fish in an even layer, seam-side down. (The wine will just cover the base of the casserole.) Cover with a lid or foil.

4 Bring to the boil, then reduce the heat and leave to simmer gently for about 10 minutes.

5 Using a slotted spoon, carefully lift the fish rolls on to a warmed serving platter.

6 Carefully strain the cooking liquor into the Light Leek Sauce and spoon a little of the sauce over the fish. Serve the remainder separately.

*155 Calories per serving*

# *L*IGHT LEEK SAUCE

40 g (1½ oz) butter
450 g (1 lb) leeks, roughly chopped
1 bunch watercress, roughly chopped
60 ml (4 tbsp) dry vermouth
284 ml (10 fl oz) carton single cream
450 ml (¾ pint) fish stock
salt and pepper

1 Melt the butter in a saucepan and add the leeks. Cover and cook for 5–6 minutes or until they are very soft. Stir in the watercress and cook for 3–4 minutes, then cool slightly.
2 Place the mixture in a food processor with the vermouth and blend for 1 minute. Add the cream and stock, season and blend again.
3 Transfer the sauce to a saucepan. Strain in the reserved fish cooking liquor, warm and serve.

*175 Calories per serving*

# *C*RISP VEGETABLE BAKE

900 g (2 lb) potatoes, peeled and chopped
salt and pepper
50 g (2 oz) butter
450 g (1 lb) cabbage, finely chopped
450 g (1 lb) carrots, peeled and roughly grated

1 Boil the potatoes in salted water for 10–15 minutes. Drain and mash with half the butter.
2 Cook the cabbage in boiling, salted water for about 5 minutes. Drain well. Stir the cabbage and carrots into the potato. Season to taste.
3 Melt the remaining butter and brush over an edged baking tray. Spread on the vegetable mixture to a depth of about 1 cm (½ inch).
4 Cook in the oven at 230°C (450°F) mark 8

for 40–45 minutes or until quite crisp on top. Serve cut into squares.

*225 Calories per serving*

# *G*LAZED LEMON PUDDINGS WITH WARM CREAM SAUCE

3 eggs
165 g (5½ oz) caster sugar
65 g (2½ oz) butter, melted
75 g (3 oz) flaked almonds
25 g (1 oz) desiccated coconut
grated rind of 1 lemon
175 ml (6 fl oz) lemon juice
175 ml (6 fl oz) milk
50 g (2 oz) plain flour
sliced pears, starfruit and grapes, to decorate

FOR THE SAUCE
450 ml (¾ pint) single cream
grated rind of 2 lemons
50 g (2 oz) caster sugar

1 Grease six 150 ml (¼ pint) ramekin dishes and line the bases with greaseproof paper.
2 Put the eggs, sugar, butter, almonds, coconut and lemon rind in a food processor and add the lemon juice, milk and flour. Blend for 1 minute. Pour into the prepared dishes and bake in the oven at 180°C (350°F) mark 4 for 45 minutes or until a light golden colour and firm.
3 Meanwhile, put the sauce ingredients in a heavy-based saucepan and bring to the boil. Boil for about 5 minutes or until thickened.
4 To serve, turn the puddings out and decorate with a few pieces of fruit. Spoon over a little of the sauce. Grill for 2–3 minutes or until lightly glazed, then serve with the remaining sauce.

*550 Calories per serving*

# NEW YEAR ELEGANCE

## Menu

*Fennel and Orange Soup*

*Beef en Croûte with Horseradish*
*Creamed Leeks and Mushrooms*
*French Beans*
*Sliced Potato Bakes*

*Crème Brûlée*

SERVES 6

We all want food to look and taste good with the minimum of effort. This menu should fit the bill. It starts with an unusual Fennel and Orange Soup, which freezes perfectly and has a subtle aniseed flavour, balanced by the taste of orange. A fillet of beef is expensive but the wonderful, juicy, tender texture justifies its cost. The Creamed Leeks and Mushrooms act as a sauce for the meat and are also a delicious vegetable. It's a bit fiddly layering the sliced potatoes into patty tins but the result is impressive. Crème Brûlée is wickedly rich; serve it with a platter of fresh strawberries, if available, or juicy mandarin oranges.

## COUNTDOWN

**The day before**

Make and purée the soup, and refrigerate, tightly covered. Prepare the orange rind; cover and refrigerate. Bake the Crème Brûlée. Cool and refrigerate, but don't grill the top yet.

*Left to right: Creamed Leeks and Mushrooms (page 125), Beef en Croûte with Horseradish (page 125), Sliced Potato Bakes (page 126)*

**On the day**

**In the morning**

Brown the fillet of beef. Wrap in pastry as directed and brush with butter. Chill until firm, then cover loosely and return to the refrigerator. Mix together the soured cream and horseradish; cover. Prepare the leeks and mushrooms; chop some parsley; top and tail 450 g (1 lb) French beans. Refrigerate all in polythene bags. Peel and slice the potatoes, and leave them soaking in cold water.

**To serve at 8 pm**

**6 pm:** Sprinkle the Crème Brûlée with sugar and grill. Return to the refrigerator until required.

**7 pm:** Preheat the oven to 230°C (450°F) mark 8. Dry the potato slices, arrange in the patty tins as directed and put in the oven to bake.

**7.30 pm:** Put the beef in the oven to bake. Cook the leeks and mushrooms; complete the sauce and keep warm, covered. Cook the beans, cover and keep warm. Check the potatoes and beef. Reheat the soup.

**8 pm:** Garnish the soup with fennel and orange and serve the meal.

---

### FREEZER NOTES

*Pack and freeze the soup. Thaw overnight at cool room temperature and reheat to serve. The remaining recipes are best not frozen.*

---

# FENNEL AND ORANGE SOUP

*For added richness, stir a little single cream into the soup before serving.*

1 large orange
salt and pepper
900 g (2 lb) Florence fennel
50 g (2 oz) butter or margarine
15 ml (1 level tbsp) plain flour
1.4 litres (2½ pints) chicken stock

1  Pare a few strips of rind from the orange and cut into very fine strips. Blanch in boiling salted water for 1 minute, drain, cool, cover and refrigerate. Grate the remaining orange rind and squeeze the juice from the orange.

2  Thinly slice the fennel, discarding the core and reserving the feathery tops.

3  Melt the butter in a large saucepan, add the fennel, cover tightly and cook gently until beginning to soften but not brown.

4  Stir in the flour and cook for 1–2 minutes before adding the stock with the grated orange rind and seasoning. Bring to the boil, cover and simmer for 20–30 minutes.

5  Cool the soup a little, then purée in a blender or food processor until quite smooth. Stir in about 90 ml (6 tbsp) orange juice, then reheat gently. Adjust the seasoning and garnish with fennel tops and pared orange rind.

*95 Calories per serving*

---

# Beef en croûte with horseradish

1 kg (2¼ lb) piece middle cut of fillet of beef
oil
3 sheets filo pastry, each measuring 25×51 cm
(10×20 inches)
50–75 g (2–3 oz) butter or margarine, melted
horseradish relish
salt and pepper
15 ml (1 level tbsp) sesame seeds
142 ml (5 fl oz) carton soured cream
watercress sprigs, to garnish

1 Trim the fillet of beef of any excess fat. Seal the meat quickly in a little hot oil in a frying pan, then cool and drain on kitchen paper.
2 Place one sheet of filo pastry on a work surface and brush lightly with melted butter. Spread over about 15 ml (1 level tbsp) horseradish. Continue layering the ingredients, ending with horseradish. Reserve some butter for glazing.
3 Place the fillet of beef on top of the pastry, season, then fold over the pastry, sealing the edges well. Trim and pinch the ends together.
4 Place the croûte, seam-side down, on a baking sheet and decorate with pastry trimmings. Brush with the remaining butter and sprinkle with sesame seeds.
5 Bake in the oven at 230°C (450°F) mark 8 for about 30 minutes, covering lightly with foil if necessary. (Place on the lower shelf in the oven, below the potatoes.) The meat should be medium-rare after this time; cook a little longer if wished.
6 Keep the croûte warm, uncovered, in a low oven. Slice the fillet and serve with the soured cream blended with horseradish relish and seasoning to taste. Garnish with watercress sprigs.

*670 Calories per serving*

# Creamed leeks and mushrooms

*The sauce is meant to be fairly thin so that this acts as an accompaniment to the beef as well as being a vegetable dish. For a little bit of added luxury, use a few wild mushrooms.*

900 g (2 lb) leeks
225 g (8 oz) button mushrooms
50 g (2 oz) butter or margarine
30 ml (2 tbsp) lemon juice
15 ml (1 level tbsp) plain flour
300 ml (½ pint) stock
30 ml (2 tbsp) single cream
chopped fresh parsley
salt and pepper

1 Trim the leeks, discarding any coarse green leaves. Split the leeks lengthways, then slice into 1 cm (½ inch) thick pieces. Wash well and drain. Wipe the mushrooms, then slice if large.
2 Heat 40 g (1½ oz) butter in a large saucepan. Add the leeks, cover tightly and cook gently for about 10 minutes or until tender but not browned.
3 Meanwhile, place the mushrooms in a small saucepan with the remaining butter and the lemon juice. Cover tightly and cook for 3–4 minutes or until the mushrooms are tender.
4 Stir the flour into the leeks, blending until smooth. Mix in the stock and bring to the boil, stirring all the time. Cook for 1–2 minutes. Stir in the mushrooms and juices and reheat gently.
5 Take the saucepan off the heat, stir in the cream and a little chopped parsley, and adjust the seasoning. Cover and keep warm in a low oven.

*120 Calories per serving*

# SLICED POTATO BAKES

*These are cooked at a high oven temperature, so keep an eye on them.*

450 g (1 lb) small old potatoes
50 g (2 oz) butter or margarine
salt and pepper

1 Peel the potatoes, then slice very thinly, preferably in a food processor. Cover the potato slices with cold water and leave to soak for at least 1 hour.
2 Drain the potatoes well and pat dry on absorbent kitchen paper.
3 Melt the butter and spoon a little into 12 patty tins. Divide the potato slices between the tins, seasoning between the layers and ending with a neat layer of potatoes. Spoon the remaining butter over the potatoes.
4 Place the potatoes at the top of the oven and bake at 230°C (450°F) mark 8 for 25–30 minutes or until well browned and tender. Ease the potato cakes out of the tins and keep warm, uncovered, in a low oven.

*115 Calories per serving*

# CRÈME BRÛLÉE

600 ml (1 pint) double cream
1 vanilla pod
4 egg yolks
125 g (4 oz) caster sugar

1 Pour the cream into the top of a double saucepan or into a heatproof bowl placed over a saucepan of simmering water. Add the vanilla pod and warm gently until almost boiling, then remove from the heat. Remove the vanilla pod.
2 Beat together the egg yolks and 50 g (2 oz) of the caster sugar until light in colour. Gradually pour on the cream, stirring until evenly mixed.
3 Stand six individual ovenproof ramekin dishes in a roasting tin containing enough hot water to come halfway up the sides of the dishes. Pour the custard mixture slowly into the ramekins, dividing it equally between them.
4 Bake in the oven at 150°C (300°F) mark 2 for about 1 hour or until set. Do not allow the skin to colour. Remove the dishes from the tin and leave to cool, then refrigerate overnight.
5 Sprinkle the remaining sugar evenly over the top of each dessert. Put under a preheated hot grill for 2–3 minutes or until the sugar turns to a caramel. Leave to cool, then chill again in the refrigerator before serving.

*575 Calories per serving*

# INDEX